# A More Perfect Union

## Essays on the Constitution

Crawford H. Greenewalt

# A More Perfect Union

## Essays on the Constitution

## *Proceedings of the American Philosophical Society* 1987

**Collected and edited by the American Philosophical Society**

New Foreword by Laurence H. Tribe

**American Philosophical Society Press**
**Philadelphia**

Transactions of the
American Philosophical Society
Held at Philadelphia
For Promoting Useful Knowledge
Volume 107, Part 4



ISBN: 978-1-60618-074-7

U.S. ISSN: 0065-9746

Library of Congress Cataloging-in-Publication Data

Names: American Philosophical Society, publisher.
Title: A more perfect union : essays on the Constitution / Proceedings of the American Philosophical Society 1987, collected and edited by the American Philosophical Society.
Description: Philadelphia : American Philosophical Society Press, 2019. | Series: Transactions of the American Philosophical Society ; Volume 107, part 4 | "Includes papers presented at two symposia held April 1987 by the American Philosophical Society in recognition of the bicentenary of the United States Constitution and also a Dr. Richard A. F. Penrose Memorial Lecture."—ECIP Preface.
Identifiers: LCCN 2019003804 | ISBN 9781606180747 (alk. paper)
Subjects: LCSH: Constitutional history—United States—Congresses.
Classification: LCC KF4541.A2 .M67 2019 | DDC 342.7302/9—dc23
LC record available at https://lccn.loc.gov/2019003804

*The American Philosophical Society respectfully dedicates this volume to Crawford H. Greenewalt, President of the Society 1984–1987*

# *Contents*



## Essays from *Proceedings of the American Philosophical Society* 1987



## Symposium on the United States Constitution

## Symposium on the Genius of the United States Constitution

# *Preface*

In April of 1987 the American Philosophical Society held two symposia in recognition of the bicentenary of the United States Constitution and heard a Penrose Lecture by a distinguished English justice on the relation of the British constitution to ours. One of these symposia, organized and moderated by Judge Arlin M. Adams, was on legal aspects of that great document; the other, organized by Arthur S. Link and moderated in his absence by Whitfield J. Bell, Jr., was on the historical aspects.

The legal scholars who spoke were Nicholas deB. Katzenbach, a former attorney general of the United States and deputy secretary of state; Geoffrey Stone, The Harry Kalven, Jr. Professor of Law at the University of Chicago; Louis Henkin, University Professor at Columbia University; and Henry Abraham, James Hart Professor of Government and Foreign Affairs, University of Virginia.

The historical scholars who spoke were Garry Wills, Henry R. Luce Professor of American Culture and Public Policy at Northwestern University; Jack P. Greene, Andrew W. Mellon Professor in the Humanities, The Johns Hopkins University; John Shy, Professor of History, University of Michigan; and Michael Kammen, Newton C. Farr Professor of American History and Culture, Cornell University.

The Penrose Lecture was delivered by Leslie Lord Scarman, the Right Honourable Lord of Appeals.

The first moderator, Arlin M. Adams, is a retired judge of the U.S. Circuit Court of Appeals and the second, Arthur S. Link, is the George Henry Davis '86 Professor of American History at Princeton University and editor of the *Papers of Woodrow Wilson.*

These talks had an importance and a timeless quality that made it seem very reasonable to publish them as a special publication of the American Philosophical Society. Furthermore, since the term of Crawford H. Greenewalt as President of this Society expired at the end of this meeting, it is fitting that we dedicate this volume to him.

It is hoped the reader will find that this set of nine complementary essays gives a very penetrating picture of the life and times of the constitutional framers as well as a considerable understanding of the problems connected with its interpretation in today's world. The reader will also gain valuable insights into the similarities and differences between our written constitution and the unwritten one of the British.

*Herman H. Goldstine*

# *Foreword: Conjugating the Constitution— From Noun to Verb*

**LAURENCE H. TRIBE***

*Carl M. Loeb University Professor and Professor of Constitutional Law, Harvard Law School*

When the American Philosophical Society held its symposia marking the 1987 bicentennial of the United States Constitution, the undertaking had a laudatory air. The talks, published at the time as collected essays and republished in this volume, celebrated the genius of the Constitution, the wisdom of its framers, and the contributions of U.S. constitutionalism to constitutional democracy worldwide. This was hardly an uncritical look—the essays engage frankly with the Constitution's structural limitations (see, e.g., Garry Wills's essay on checks on power and Nicholas Katzenbach's piece on the resulting need for creativity in the political process); its shortcomings as an instrument of popular sovereignty (especially Louis Henkin's examination of the Constitution as social compact and Michael Kammen's assessment of the Constitution as a "living document"); and the outsized role of historical happenstance in the instrument's drafting (see, for instance, John Shy's and Jack Greene's insightful contributions on the historical context of the Constitutional Convention in Philadelphia). But the overall impression one derives from the essays is that, viewed in snapshot in 1987, the American constitutional system works pretty well.

*I want to thank Annie Hollister, J.D. 2020, for her excellent—and indispensable—assistance with this Foreword. All errors, of course, are mine.

If that impression feels somewhat inapposite in 2019, that is because, for all its longevity, our Constitution is far from being a constant. Reading these essays today, one can't help being struck by the revolutionary ways in which "the Constitution" has evolved and been transformed in the third of a century since the bicentennial, even though the only amendment to the document since 1987 is a relatively minor one proposed in 1789 and finally ratified in 1992.[1] The constitutional snapshot framed in the bicentennial essays—which provide both illuminating historical analysis tied to the problems facing a modern nation and incisive responses to the leading constitutional debates of the time—stands in dramatic contrast with the constitutional videoclip with which APS would surely wish to observe its own 275th Anniversary. Indeed, what we mean by "the Constitution" isn't only the document we *call* the Constitution, but also the constitutional law, discourse, and debate that shape our understanding of and experience with that document.[2] *This* Constitution cannot be captured in a snapshot. In reflecting on that contrast, I think the best way to capture the apparent gulf between our constitutional discourse then and now is to reframe our conception of what, in its essence, the Constitution *is*. The Constitution is not a thing, fixed in time and space except on the rare occasions when its language is formally amended. It is, rather, an ongoing action, a work both in and of progress. The Constitution, never quite properly captured in a noun, now surely must be understood as a verb.

* * *

This dynamic understanding of the Constitution is embedded in the founders' project.[3] The commitment to active progress is reflected in our canonical texts, from the Declaration of Independence's demand that government reflect the needs and desires of the governed ("Governments are instituted among Men, deriving their just powers from the consent of the governed,— . . . whenever any Form of Government becomes destructive of these ends, itis the right of the People to alter or abolish it"),[4] to the aspirations expressed

---

[1] See U.S. const. amend. XXVII (requiring that any increases to congressional pay take effect only after an intervening election).

[2] For more discussion on this point, see Akhil Reed Amar, "The Supreme Court, 1999 Term—Foreword: The Document and the Doctrine," 114 *Harv. L. Rev.* 26 (2000).

[3] See Richard H. Fallon, *The Dynamic Constitution: An Introduction to American Constitutional Law* (New York: Cambridge University Press, 2004).

[4] The Declaration of Independence para. 2 (1776).

in the Constitution's Preamble ("a *more* perfect Union"),[5] to Lincoln's reframing of our national values at Gettysburg ("the *unfinished work* which they who fought here have thus far so nobly advanced").[6] The 1987 essays included here, when read today, illustrate the ways in which jurisprudence has evolved and point to directions in which we must continue to lay new tracks. In the decades intervening since the Constitution's bicentennial, new threats to the constitutional project have arisen, and existing cracks have become more visible.

Notably, our assumptions about who is entitled to a voice in the conversation have undergone major transformations. To some, it might be unsurprising that a panel of constitutional experts assembled in 1987 would have been composed entirely of white men who (for the most part) shared consistent, or at least readily reconcilable, worldviews. But the consequence of this composition is that the portrait of our constitutional republic, viewed from several decades later, looks strikingly incomplete. Were the authors of these symposium essays to gather today, it is hard to imagine that they would be willing to present the legacy of slavery and the subjugation of indigenous people as aberrations best relegated to a distant past. Rather, the expansion of who is included in the conversation has forced intellectual discourse about our Constitution to more fully appreciate the ways in which these horrors have not merely marred our history but powerfully shaped our institutional structures; slavery, in particular, was intentionally and explicitly incorporated into our national design, and informed the architecture of the United States Congress and the Electoral College.

It is tempting to ascribe our increased social and political emphasis on questions of racism, misogyny, and homophobia to a changing demographic landscape. It is certainly true that, as awareness of these evils has become more central to the *cultural* discourse, our *constitutional* discourse has been steered in new directions. But, of course, this awareness is hardly new to those who have experienced constitutionally sanctioned oppression from the moment of the nation's birth. The same year that the essays in this collection were originally published, Justice Thurgood Marshall delivered his own reflections on the Constitution's bicentennial, in a landmark address to (of all things)

[5] U.S. const. preamble (emphasis added).

[6] Abraham Lincoln, The Gettysburg Address (1863) (emphasis added). One of the contributors to this volume, Garry Wills, has provided a brilliant exegesis of Lincoln's use of the Declaration in remaking our national self-definition at Gettysburg. See Garry Wills, *Linclon at Gettysburg: The Words That Remade America* (New York: Touchstone, 1992).

the San Francisco Patent and Trademark Law Association.[7] Pointing to the Constitution's intentional protection of slavery, and to its exclusion of women and nonpropertied people from the polity, Justice Marshall observed the bicentennial by "commemorat[ing] the suffering, struggle, and sacrifice that has triumphed over much of what was wrong with the original document, and observ[ing] the anniversary with hopes not realized and promises not fulfilled."[8] I echoed this sentiment in a commencement address delivered later that month, in which I suggested that, "the *real* framers of our Constitution were not only the propertied, white gentlemen who met in Philadelphia, but the many more . . . who marched and bled, who sang and rode buses and sat in and sometimes died, to make freedom ring."[9]

At the same time, the past three decades have seen a remarkable shift when it comes to cultural and social awareness of sexual orientation and gender identity. This shift, in turn, has been accompanied by an almost-unimaginable transformation in jurisprudence. Writing just a year after *Bowers v. Hardwick*,[10] the now-defunct Supreme Court case upholding the criminalization of sodomy (and gratuitously focusing on the same-sex character of consensual adult intimacy despite the sex-neutral character of the state law at issue), the contributors to these bicentennial essays could hardly have anticipated the rapid progression of the LGBTQ-rights movement, which, through targeted legal initiatives, has succeeded in broadening the scope of the Fourteenth Amendment as interpreted by the Supreme Court.

The importance of recognizing these sociocultural blind spots of 1987 is not superficial. As Michael Kammen's essay points out, constitutional discourse evolves in step with changing conceptions of popular sovereignty and human flourishing; recognizing changes to the latter is essential to understanding the ways in which the former has changed in the years since the Constitution's bicentennial. The rapid (at least in constitutional terms) development of the Supreme Court's gay-rights jurisprudence is a prime example of this transforma-

---

[7] See Thurgood Marshall, Commentary, "Reflections on the Bicentennial of the United States Constitution," 101 *Harv. L. Rev.* 1 (1987).

[8] Id. at 5.

[9] Laurence H. Tribe, "Bicentennial Blues: To Praise the Constitution or to Bury It?" 37 *Am. U. L. Rev.* 1, 4 (1987).

[10] 478 U.S. 186 (1986). In the interest of disclosure: I argued the losing side of this case before the Supreme Court, fully expecting to lose narrowly but hoping to generate dissents that would eventually become law. The 5-4 outcome, with powerful dissents by Justices Harry Blackmun and John Paul Stevens, joined by Justices William J. Brennan and Thurgood Marshall, vindicated that hope.

tion. *Bowers*, of course, has been overturned by *Lawrence v. Texas*.[11] But it is the landmark marriage-equality cases, *United States v. Windsor*[12] and *Obergefell v. Hodges*,[13] that best demonstrate the parallel progression of cultural awareness and constitutional jurisprudence. These cases did more than simply extend Fourteenth Amendment protections to the previously unrecognized class of LGBTQ Americans by shielding intimate practices associated with that class from state criminalization; Justice Anthony Kennedy's analysis in those cases, with its centering of "equal dignity" at the heart of legal protections, encompassed an affirmative right to participate without discrimination in the state's secular endorsement of a religious and social institution (there, the institution of marriage) and expanded our understanding of the Fourteenth Amendment itself.[14]

* * *

*Windsor* was the bellwether of another doctrinal shift that might have surprised scholars writing at the time of the bicentennial: the increasing embrace of federalism—once almost synonymous with resistance to desegregation and the full citizenship of African Americans—by the political left. State resistance to overbearing federal oversight is nothing new, but the decades following the Constitution's bicentennial have seen the growth of a particularly thick species of federalism. A line of Supreme Court cases beginning with *New York v. United States*[15] and including *Printz v. United States*[16] and *Murphy*

---

[11] 539 U.S. 558 (2003). Again, in the interest of full disclosure: I wrote the brief for and was counsel of record in this case for the American Civil Liberties Union, whose position that *Bowers* should be overruled—and declared wrong from the day it was decided—ultimately prevailed. Although the state statute at issue in this case, unlike that at issue in *Bowers*, criminalized only same-sex sodomy—a feature on which Justice Sandra Day O'Connor focused in limiting her concurrence to such discriminatory laws—the majority opinion, written by Justice Anthony Kennedy, deemed it necessary to explain why not even broadening the state's ban to cover all sodomy would save it from invalidation, given the equation in public consciousness between banning consensual sodomy and branding all sexually active gays, lesbians, and bisexuals as criminals, thereby justifying other measures discriminating against members of the LGBTQ community.

[12] 570 U.S. 744 (2013).

[13] 135 S. Ct. 2584 (2015).

[14] For a fuller discussion on these cases and the evolution of "equal dignity," see Laurence H. Tribe, "*Lawrence v. Texas*: The 'Fundamental Right' that Dare Not Speak Its Name," 117 *Harv. L. Rev.* 1893 (2004); Kenji Yoshino, "The New Equal Protection," 124 *Harv. L. Rev.* 747 (2011); Laurence H. Tribe, "Equal Dignity: Speaking Its Name," 129 *Harv. L. Rev.* F. 16 (2015).

[15] 505 U.S. 144 (1992) (striking down a federal law compelling individual states to choose between two exercises of sovereign lawmaking power—taking title to the nuclear waste within their borders or adopting a federally approved regulatory scheme for radioactive material—neither of which Congress could constitutionally require states to undertake).

[16] 521 U.S. 898 (1997) (striking down portions of the Brady Act, a federal gun-control statute, that imposed a national system of background checks for handgun sales, on the grounds that the Act unconstitutionally compelled state actors to carry out federal law).

*v. NCAA*[17] have interpreted the Tenth Amendment to sharply limit the federal government's power to compel states to carry out a federal policy agenda.

Although this jurisprudence has emerged from the opinions of conservative justices, its reasoning has been adopted by the champions of progressive causes.[18] *Windsor*'s federalism-based rebuke of the Defense of Marriage Act provides an excellent illustration.[19] More recently, the "anti-commandeering" reasoning that fueled *New York v. United States* and *Printz* has found its way into lower-court opinions upholding protections for so-called sanctuary cities,[20] and will likely continue to reappear as blue states continue to resist the agenda of the distinctly nonblue Trump presidency.

The "thickening" of federalism jurisprudence has also spurred a renewed (or, for many, entirely new) attentiveness to the interplay between the United States Constitution and its less-celebrated state counterparts.[21] This has been especially salient in the context of what might seem a surprising about-face to constitutional scholars writing at the end of the twentieth century—an about-face rooted in a discontented citizenry's increasing interest in employing state mechanisms to protect from the federal judiciary such basic rights as the right to vote. That turnabout sits in stark contrast to minority groups' historical reliance on the federal judiciary to protect such rights from states. This trend is partly a product of necessity, given the ever-stronger grip of partisan gerry-

---

[17] 138 S. Ct. 1461 (2018) (striking down a federal law prohibiting amateur sports betting on the grounds that it "unequivocally dictate[d] what state legislatures may and may not do." Id. at 1478).

[18] This rise in so-called "progressive federalism" is attributable in no small part to the scholarship of Yale Law School Dean Heather Gerken. See, e.g., Heather Gerken, "The Supreme Court, 2009 Term—Foreword: Federalism All the Way Down," 124 *Harv. L. Rev.* 4 (2010).

[19] The Act barred same-sex couples whose marriages had been legally recognized at the state level from receiving federal income tax and other financial benefits available to those in heterosexual marriages. In his majority opinion, Justice Kennedy relied on the fact that this exercise of federal power departed sharply from a long tradition in which federal tax laws simply absorbed each state's definition of family relationships like marriage, including the state's age and other requirements for entering into such relationships. The majority opinion treated that departure not as unconstitutional in itself but as requiring a more searching inquiry into the government's explanations for the departure. In the instance of the Defense of Marriage Act, Justice Kennedy's opinion concluded, the post-hoc explanations were mere pretexts for the real reason Congress carved out an exception for same-sex marriage: to relegate same-sex relationships to a distinctly second-class status, which the Court held an impermissible purpose with an impermissible effect. See *United States v. Windsor*, 570 U.S. 744, 766–74 (2013).

[20] See, e.g., *County of Santa Clara v. Trump*, 275 F. Supp. 3d 1196, 1215–16 (N.D. Cal. 2017) (enjoining the enforcement of an Executive Order that threatened to withdraw federal funds from municipalities that refused to enforce federal immigration law, on the grounds that the order unconstitutionally conscripts local law enforcement entities into executing a federal regulatory scheme); see also Renée Loth, "'Sanctuary Cities' Have the Law on Their Side," *Bos. Globe* (Mar. 6, 2017) https://www.bostonglobe.com/opinion/2017/03/06/sanctuary-cities-have-law-their-side/AAmVsF94Jw2IXATCOXv9PN/story.html.

[21] For a splendid account of the relationship between state constitutional law and federal constitutional jurisprudence, see Jeffrey Sutton, *51 Imperfect Solutions* (New York: Oxford University Press, 2018).

mandering and the Supreme Court's apparent reluctance to take concrete steps to protect the integrity of our nation's elections.[22] In the face of these frustrations, interested parties have sought—with notable early success—to implement state-based solutions, including the invalidation of Pennsylvania's partisan district map by that state's highest court on state constitutional grounds[23] and, in Arizona, appointing an independent redistricting commission via referendum.[24]

It is, of course, possible for states to take their protected power too far, such that the exercise of state autonomy (or, as Justice Kennedy liked to put it, state *dignity*)[25] becomes an interference with federally guaranteed individual rights. The delicate balance between state and national interests has been a central challenge of the American constitutional project from the beginning (as John Shy's essay reminds us), but recent decades have sharpened this challenge in new and transformative ways.

* * *

Alongside substantive jurisprudential changes, the last thirty years have seen the flowering of a veritable cornucopia of interpretive modes. Perhaps most notable is the maturation of so-called originalism, which appears in these pages as a nascent idea worthy of further exploration (see Michael Kammen's essay). And explorers have certainly taken note, as discourse around originalist interpretation has shifted in focus from the original-intention jurisprudence

---

[22] We saw this in the 2017 Term's decision in *Gill v. Whitford*, 138 S. Ct. 1916 (2018), in which the Supreme Court declined to reach the merits of a partisan gerrymandering claim, on the reasoning that the parties had not properly shown that they had suffered injury; and, somewhat differently, in *Shelby County v. Holder*, 570 U.S. 529 (2013), in which the Supreme Court severely weakened the protective pre-clearance provisions of the Voting Rights Act of 1965.

[23] See *League of Women Voters of Pennsylvania v. Commonwealth*, 181 A.3d 1083 (Pa. 2018), cert. denied sub nom. *Turzai v. League of Women Voters of Pennsylvania*, 138 S. Ct. 1323 (2018). Efforts by the losing parties to make a federal case out of it, as it were, failed utterly, as the U.S. Supreme Court rebuffed their petitions for review without comment.

[24] See *Ariz. State Legislature v. Ariz. Indep. Districting Comm'n*, 135 S. Ct. 46 (2015). The Supreme Court's opinion for a bare majority, written by Justice Ruth Bader Ginsburg, ingeniously treated the state's electorate as its "legislature" for the purpose at hand, thereby avoiding the dissenting Justices' quite plausible charge that Arizona had violated the federal constitutional requirement that congressional district lines be drawn by the relevant state's "legislature." See U.S. const. art. 1, § 4. Illustrating how the verb-like character of the Constitution need not always bend its trajectory toward justice, it seems unlikely that the Court as currently composed would reach the same conclusion, and it is at least plausible that it would, in an appropriate case, overrule this 5-4 precedent.

[25] See, e.g., *Idaho v. Coeur d'Alene Tribe of Idaho*, 521 U.S. 261, 287 (1997).

of former Attorney General Edwin Meese[26] to the original-public-meaning analysis championed by Justice Antonin Scalia[27] and constitutional scholar Jack Balkin,[28] which has come to enjoy widespread acceptance in the scholarly mainstream. Today, "originalism," once associated exclusively with the likes of Judge Robert Bork,[29] is quite reasonably understood—despite the determined opposition of the late Justice Scalia[30]—to include living, progressive varieties.[31]

The evolution of constitutional jurisprudence in response to shifting intellectual currents and cultural norms is not limited to the development of new modes of analysis. The result is the dramatic visibility in 2019 of dangers not readily foreseeable in 1987, and the re-emergence of ideas previously thought dead, and now properly understood as having merely been dormant.

First on this unhappy list is the fulfillment of Justice Robert H. Jackson's ominous prophecy, in his dissent in *Korematsu v. United States*,[32] that the Supreme Court's willingness to rationalize and ultimately uphold racist military orders would invite future leaders to overstep the bounds of the Constitution, and future Courts to uphold such oversteps.[33] Notwithstanding Chief Justice John Roberts's insistence to the contrary,[34] the 2018 decision in *Trump v. Hawaii*,[35] upholding the third iteration of the Trump administration's anti-Muslim travel ban, provided an example of exactly the type of judicial blessing for bigoted executive action that Justice Jackson anticipated. As Justice Sonia Sotomayor made clear in her blistering dissent, in "blindly accepting the Government's misguided invitation to sanction a discriminatory policy motivated by animosity toward a disfavored group, all in the name of a superficial

---

[26] See, e.g., Edwin Meese, Speech Before the American Bar Association (Jul. 9, 1985) https://www.justice.gov/sites/default/files/ag/legacy/2011/08/23/07-09-1985.pdf.

[27] See Antonin Scalia, *A Matter of Interpretation: Federal Courts and the Law* (Princeton, NJ: Princeton University Press, 1997).

[28] See, e.g., Jack M. Balkin, "Original Meaning and Constitutional Redemption," 24 *Const. Comment.* 427 (2007).

[29] See Robert H. Bork, *The Tempting of America* (New York: Touchstone, 1990).

[30] See Scalia, supra note 27, at 37–47. I should note that Justice Scalia and I enjoyed a rich debate on this point. See Laurence H. Tribe, Comment, in Scalia, supra note 27, at 65–94; Antonin Scalia, Response, in Scalia, supra note 27, at 133–143.

[31] For a probing analysis of the relationship between originalism and progressivism, see Jack M. Balkin, *Living Originalism* (Cambridge, MA: Belknap Press, 2011).

[32] 323 U.S. 214 (1944). Korematsu has had a lasting jurisprudential legacy as the first case to purportedly apply "the most rigid scrutiny" to race-based government action. Id. at 216. This application of supposedly strict scrutiny in fact led the Court to uphold executive orders excluding American citizens of Japanese ancestry from designated areas of the West Coast and forcing those Americans, on the basis of race, to leave their homes and belongings. The Court, while claiming to subject the government's actions and justifications to strict scrutiny, manifested an alarming deference to factual assertions that proved, in retrospect, to have been not just incorrect but fabricated.

[33] See id. at 246 (Jackson, J., dissenting).

[34] See *Trump v. Hawaii*, 138 S. Ct. 2392, 2423 (2018).

[35] 138 S. Ct. 2392.

claim of national security, the Court redeploy[ed] the same dangerous logic underlying *Korematsu*."[36]

Recent decades have also seen the reflowering of *Plessy v. Ferguson*'s[37] blindness to the realities of racial oppression. This willful rejection of the realities of American racism, typified by Chief Justice Roberts's opinion in in *Parents Involved in Community Schools v. Seattle School District* ("The way to stop discrimination on the basis of race is to stop discriminating on the basis of race"),[38] foreshadows the impending death of all public programs that take the race of individuals into account, even individually and holistically, in allocating opportunities, while ignoring the undeniable truism that layering neutrality atop systemic inequality serves only to perpetuate that inequality.

So, too, have recent years seen the recrudescence of a kind of neo-*Lochnerism*[39] in *Citizens United v. FEC*[40] and *Janus v. AFSCME*[41]—cases in which the Supreme Court employed notions of "free speech" (as opposed to the due process "liberty-of-contract" language employed in *Lochner*), uninflected by concern with equality or with democracy, to uphold systemic injustice and the maldistribution of wealth and political power.[42] These developing notions of free speech have, of course, emerged from a Supreme Court reacting to the political crises and controversies of its time, and in that sense are familiar in form—if not in substance—when viewed through the lens of Geoffrey Stone's essay on the evolution of free expression jurisprudence.

To confuse matters, the deployment of an apparently supercharged and one-dimensional First Amendment has occurred alongside an erosion of the antiestablishment principle once thought central to both the religious liberty

---

[36] Id. at 2448 (Sotomayor, J., dissenting).

[37] 163 U.S. 537 (1896) (upholding "separate but equal" public facilities for whites and people of color).

[38] 551 U.S. 701, 748 (2007) (holding that Equal Protection prohibited Seattle public schools from taking race into account when assigning students to oversubscribed schools).

[39] See *Lochner v. New York*, 198 U.S. 45 (1905) (striking down a New York law regulating the hours of bakery workers on the grounds that labor regulation violated the substantive due process right to liberty of contract).

[40] 558 U.S. 310 (2010) (holding that corporate funding of political messaging is protected speech under the First Amendment and striking down a federal statute restricting corporate spending promoting or opposing particular candidates in connection with federal elections).

[41] 138 S. Ct. 2448 (2018) (striking down a state law requiring public-sector employees who are represented by a union to pay "agency fees" to support collective bargaining, on the grounds that required fees are unconstitutional compelled speech under the First Amendment).

[42] See Kathleen M. Sullivan, Comment, "Two Concepts of Freedom of Speech," 124 *Harv. L. Rev.* 143 (2010) (articulating the distinction between an "egalitarian" vision of free speech—which demands that considerations of political equality and distributive justice be incorporated into First Amendment jurisprudence—and a "libertarian" vision of the same right—which views the First Amendment purely as a check on government intervention in the marketplace of ideas). For further insight into the role of free speech in shaping social order, see Robert C. Post, *Citizens Divided: Campaign Finance Reform and the Constitution* (Cambridge, MA: Harvard University Press, 2014).

and the secular governance promised by that same Amendment. From cases like *Burwell v. Hobby Lobby Stores*[43] and *Town of Greece v. Galloway*[44]—in which the Supreme Court upheld a town's practice of opening board meetings with a prayer—to the 2017 Term's twinned-yet-ill-matched *Trump v. Hawaii* and *Masterpiece Cakeshop v. Colorado Civil Rights Commission*;[45] and from the Court's 5-4 approval of the execution of Dominique Ray by the state of Alabama without allowing Ray the comfort of an imam's presence to administer last rites[46]—a picture emerges of an Establishment Clause that provides unwavering support to some, but provides shockingly weak protection to those who may need it the most.

* * *

These are themes that a commentator on the Constitution writing at the time of the bicentennial might have found unfamiliar—or extinct. Even more alarming to such a commentator would be the emergence, in the first quarter of the twenty-first century, of new structural perils to the constitutional project, and the subsequent development of new foci within the field of constitutional law.

The dramatically antidemocratic consequences of the slavery-grounded Electoral College became inescapably clear in the presidential elections of 2000, 2004, and 2016; one result has been the new exploration of workarounds to this (previously only theoretically) flawed anachronism, such as the National Popular Vote Interstate Compact[47]—a scheme by which, once enough states have signed on to guarantee the winning total of 270 electoral votes, signed-on states would agree to cast all of their electoral votes for whichever presidential

---

[43] 134 S. Ct. 2751 (2014) (holding that employers could not be required to provide contraceptive healthcare coverage in contravention of sincerely held religious beliefs).

[44] 134 S. Ct. 1811 (2014).

[45] 138 S. Ct. 419 (2018) (in which the Court held that antireligious statements by a member of the Colorado Civil Rights Commission constituted a violation of the Free Exercise rights of a baker who was facing a disciplinary hearing in front of the Commission for refusing to bake a wedding cake for a same-sex couple); cf. *Trump v. Hawaii*, 138 S. Ct. 2392 (2018) (in which the Court held that anti-Muslim statements by the President of the United States prior to the promulgation of an exclusionary travel ban did not implicate a violation of the Establishment Clause of the First Amendment).

[46] See *Dunn v. Ray*, 139 S. Ct. 661 (2019) (mem.). It was undisputed that the state would have permitted a Christian minister to accompany the convict into the death chamber, but made no provision for clergy of other faiths to play that final role. Justice Elena Kagan forcefully argued in her dissent that the Court's callous dismissal of Ray's claim of religious discrimination violated the "clearest command" of the First Amendment's Establishment clause, id. at 661 (quoting Larson v. Valente, 456 U.S. 228, 244 [1982]), with little justification beyond a desire to meet the state's preferred execution date. See id. at 662.

[47] Professors (and brothers) Vikram Amar and Akhil Reed Amar have been notable champions of this plan. See, e.g., Vikram David Amar, "(Unpersuasive) Challenges to the National Popular Vote Plan: Part One in a Series of Columns," *Verdict* (Mar. 15, 2013) https://verdict.justia.com/2013/03/15/unpersuasive-challenges-to-the-national-popular-vote-plan.

candidate wins the national popular vote.[48] Also pressing on the constitutional psyche are the huge distortions caused by increasingly sophisticated partisan gerrymandering and the confluence of forces, including technological transformations in media (social and otherwise) that have given rise to previously unimagined constitutional issues and conflicts—ultimately making possible the rise to power of as norm-breaking and democracy-threatening a President as Donald J. Trump.

The increasing visibility of these fissures in our constitutional foundation has fostered the re-emergence of constitutional provisions either long forgotten (like the Second Amendment and the Foreign Emoluments Clause[49]), unused for decades (like the Impeachments Clause and the 25th Amendment, which was added to the Constitution only as of 1967[50]), or seemingly dead (like the 27th Amendment,[51] finally ratified in 1992, or the Equal Rights Amendment,[52] assumed dead as of 1982 but still arguably percolating through the states). Upheavals in the composition of the Supreme Court have exacerbated this constitutional unease. The Court's increasingly tumultuous appointment process—stratospherically departed from the rosy picture painted in Henry Abraham's essay—has eroded public trust in the institution, beginning with Justice Lewis Powell's resignation and the failed nominations of Judges Robert Bork and Douglas Ginsburg, and far from finished with Justice Brett Kavanaugh's electrifyingly divisive appointment in 2018.

The discussions orbiting around these changes have further blurred the always somewhat artificial and inescapably elusive line between constitutional law and constitutional politics, which has become increasingly contested as constitutional terms like "high Crimes and Misdemeanors"[53] and "constitutional crisis" saturate public discourse. Incessant impeachment talk distorts public consciousness by obscuring legitimate objects of outrage and stoking the flames of partisan polarization into a full-on blaze of tribalism.[54] Likewise, crisis talk transmutes political flashpoints into existential threats while dulling

---

[48] As of this writing, in March 2019, the Compact has been signed into law in thirteen jurisdictions, including the District of Columbia, with a total of 181 electoral votes.

[49] U.S. Const. art. I, § 9, cl. 8.

[50] U.S. Const. amend. XXV (providing for the sidelining of a President who is deemed "unable to discharge the powers and duties of his office." Id. § 3).

[51] Supra note 1.

[52] Proposed Amendment to the Constitution of the United States, H.R.J. res. 208, 92d Cong., 2d Sess., 86 Stat. 1523 (1972) ("Equality of rights under the law shall not be denied or abridged by the United States or by any State on account of sex." Id. § 1).

[53] U.S. Const. art. II, § 4.

[54] See Joshua Matz & Laurence H. Tribe, "America Is Too Impeachment Obsessed," *The Atlantic* (Feb. 22, 2019) https://www.theatlantic.com/ideas/archive/2019/02/why-democrats-shouldnt-talk-about-impeaching-trump/583195/; see also Laurence H. Tribe and Joshua Matz, *To End A Presidency: The Power of Impeachment* (New York: Basic Books, 2018).

the capacity of observers to recognize real dangers when they do arise. Meanwhile, contemplation of calling an Article V constitutional convention, previously all-but-unimaginable, has crept into the discursive mainstream.

This line-blurring is embodied in the rise of what Professor Mark Tushnet has called "constitutional hardball"[55]—that is, the willingness of political actors to strain the bounds of constitutional norms while remaining squarely within the realm of permissible constitutional doctrine. This incendiary brand of constitutional gamesmanship has been employed ever more frequently in the decades following the Constitution's bicentennial, escalating sharply with the impeachment of President William Jefferson Clinton in 1998 and reaching new heights with the Senate's sabotage of Judge Merrick Garland's nomination to the Supreme Court in 2016, with the Senate's Republican majority refusing even to meet with President Obama's nominee, much less give him a hearing and an up-or-down vote, to fill the vacancy created by Justice Scalia's sudden death 269 days before the next presidential election. For much of this time, Republican officeholders have been notably more adept at employing the Constitution's mechanisms in this way—which has left Democrats struggling to keep up, while also grappling with the antidemocratic consequences of taking these tactics too far.[56]

Since the mid-twentieth century, analysis of the separation of powers between the executive and legislative branches has been constructed not around the constitutional text, nor even binding Supreme Court precedent, but rather around Justice Jackson's concurring opinion in *Youngstown Sheet & Tube Co. v. Sawyer*,[57] which measured the legitimacy of presidential conduct along the two dimensions of the President's independent authority to act, on the one hand, and congressional approval or disapproval of the President's conduct, on the other. In the three-quarters of a century since, courts have tended to resolve apparent conflicts between Congress and the President by mapping those conflicts onto *Youngstown*'s two-dimensional landscape.

This elegant topography, which purports to fill in a constitutional gap regarding the scope of executive authority, in truth provides little guidance about how to assess presidential action when Congress has neither specifically

---

[55] See Mark Tushnet, "Constitutional Hardball," 37 *J. Marshall L. Rev.* 523 (2004).

[56] See Joseph Fishkin & David E. Pozen, Essay, "Asymmetric Constitutional Hardball," 118 *Colum. L. Rev.* 915 (2018); Jed H. Shugerman, "Constitutional Hardball v. Beanball: Identifying Fundamentally Antidemocratic Tactics," 119 *Colum. L. Rev. Online* (forthcoming 2019).

[57] 343 U.S. 579 (1952) (Jackson, J., concurring) (condemning President Truman's seizure of the U.S. steel industry during the Korean war).

or impliedly authorized—nor specifically or impliedly prohibited—the presidential conduct in question. Telling us nothing about how to resolve disputes falling within what Justice Jackson famously called this "zone of twilight,"[58] by which he meant the zone between implied (or explicit) authorization and implied (or explicit) prohibition, that canonical opinion also tells us precious little about how to go about deciding what Congress has "implied" by its silence; when to read either an implied green light or an implied red light in what Congress almost, but not quite, enacted as law; or how to justify giving legal effect to congressional hints that do not have the form of lawmaking required by Article I, Section 7, of the Constitution.[59]

Furthermore, the shadow of *Youngstown* has encouraged courts to organize conflicts over presidential power around largely descriptive principles of separation of powers, often giving short shrift to the questions of individual rights that animate those conflicts.[60] This omission becomes more salient—and disturbing—as courts increasingly construe congressional and constitutional ambiguities as granting an expansive grant of authority to the executive.[61] This trend, coupled with a judicial reluctance (Ninth Amendment notwithstanding)[62] to expand the stable of recognized individual rights, risks losing sight of the

---

[58] Id. at 637.

[59] These questions are at the center of the dispute created by President Trump's declaration of a national emergency at the U.S.–Mexico border and his veto of the congressional override of that declaration. In order for the declaration to survive scrutiny under *Youngstown*, the President's supporters would need, among other things, to explain how Congress's override, in conjunction with the history of the dispute, does not imply legislative disapproval of the President's actions despite the override's failure to become law by virtue of the President's veto. See Jennifer Rubin, "How You Slow Down a Wannabe Authoritarian," *Wash. Post* (Mar. 15, 2019, 10:15 AM) https://www.washingtonpost.com/opinions/2019/03/15/how-you-slow-down-wanna-be-authoritarian/?utm_term=.02f422155fb6; see also Laurence Tribe, "Trump's 'Emergency' Is Already Doing Serious Harm. Courts Must End It If Congress Can't," *USA Today* (Mar. 14, 2019, 3:56 PM) https://www.usatoday.com/story/opinion/2019/03/14/senate-vote-trump-emergency-serious-harm-courts-congress-end-it-column/3161198002/. In the interest of full disclosure: I am currently representing the City of El Paso in litigation against the President related to this question.

[60] See Laurence H. Tribe, "Transcending the Youngstown Triptych: A Multidimensional Reappraisal of Separation of Powers Doctrine," 126 *Yale L. J. F.* 86 (2016). These challenges have emerged in the context of deafening constitutional and congressional silences that implicate both structural puzzles (for instance, about the limits of executive power or the scope of Congress's authority to preempt state prerogatives) and individual rights (especially with respect to whether and when to recognize new rights). As Lord Scarman's essay points out, silences of this nature—especially about the scope of institutional powers—invite judges to fill in the gaps, inevitably giving rise to competing approaches to construing those silences. See Laurence H. Tribe, "Soundings and Silences," in *The Invisible Constitution in Comparative Perspective*, edited by Rosalind Dixon and Adrienne Stone (New York: Cambridge University Press, 2018).

[61] See, e.g., *Zivotofsky v. Kerry*, 135 S. Ct. 2076 (2015). *Zivotofsky* construed the Constitution's Reception Clause, U.S. const. art. II, § 3 (granting the President the power to receive foreign ambassadors), as giving the President exclusive power to recognize foreign states and to determine which state may claim a contested region or city as its capital, see *Zivotofsky*, 135 S. Ct. at 2087.

[62] U.S. const. amend. IX ("The enumeration in the Constitution, of certain rights, shall not be construed to deny or disparage others retained by the people.").

Constitution's fundamental mission of creating and protecting a government for the people.

* * *

Our nation's canonical texts express aspirations of growth, innovation, and dynamic responsiveness to the evolving needs of "We the People." The most pressing constitutional question today is just how vulnerable those aspirations are to the vagaries of human character.

The framers could not have foreseen the developments in politics and technology that created the present constitutional moment. They were conscious that they had created a Constitution that would operate as a verb. But not even they could have imagined what its conjugation might portend. We are experiencing a close encounter with democratic collapse and the rise of authoritarianism in the person of President Trump—who is best understood as symptom no less than cause. Is it possible that the Constitution's structurally flawed guardrails will not hold, or will prove insufficient to prevent the irreversible deformation of democracy into kleptocracy, autocracy, or even dictatorship?

We can't pretend to be able to answer this question anytime soon. But my gamble is that, if we treat this moment as an invaluable learning opportunity and not as an inevitable harbinger of constitutional doom, our noble experiment in government of the people, by the people, for the people will not, in Lincoln's immortal words, perish from the earth.

# *Remarks*

## *Bicentennial Blues: To Praise the Constitution or to Bury It?**

**LAURENCE H. TRIBE****

*Carl M. Loeb University Professor and Professor of Constitutional Law, Harvard Law School*

I am deeply grateful for your decision to confer an honorary degree upon me today. And I am delighted that you have invited me to address you on the occasion of your commencement. Let me congratulate you on all that you have achieved. You have the special privilege of commencing in the year of the Constitution's Bicentennial—and within several thousand yards of the Constitution itself—a document that travelled by stagecoach, at 11:00 in the morning on September 18, 1787, from Philadelphia to New York. It was spirited to Virginia in a linen sack to save it from the advancing British in August 1814. For many years, it was stored in an old green cabinet with seven ancient swords in a basement not very far from here. It now rests in the National Archives. It has had a colorful trajectory.

As your careers follow their own trajectories, taking you far from today's celebration, you may find yourselves, from time to time, in a position roughly like that of the pilgrims in one of my favorite cartoons. Two of them stand on a boat—it appears to be the *Mayflower*. They scan the distant horizon. As they catch a glimpse of land, one says to the other, "Religious freedom is my immediate objective . . . but my long-term goal is to go into real estate." You might ponder that throughout your careers.



**This is an unrevised transcription of Professor Tribe's Commencement Address delivered on May 17, 1987, at the American University Washington College of Law Commencement at the John F. Kennedy Center for the Performing Arts, Washington, DC, published in 37 *American University Law Review* 1.

It is no wonder that a cynic said not too long ago, "America is not merely a city on a hill, it is also a city on the make." My wish for you is that your lives, whether in the law or outside the law, might to some degree deny the cynic's prognosis. But I am not here to urge all of you to pursue paths of pure self-sacrifice and unalloyed civic virtue. I have no illusions about the possibility of that, and I would be a hypocrite if I protested too much about pursuits that have at least some worldly dimension. After all, my own Supreme Court arguments have included cases, such as *Pennzoil v. Texaco*, as well as civil rights and civil liberties disputes. But it may not be too much to urge you all to dedicate yourselves, at least in some small part, to keeping the Constitution's spirit alive. With that end in view, I am calling my brief remarks this morning, "Bicentennial Blues: To Praise the Constitution or to Bury It?"

During your law school years, you have encountered at least two radically different visions of what it might mean to praise and to perpetuate the Constitution. One vision is propounded principally by Attorney General Edwin Meese, who proclaims the sanctity of the original Constitution of 1787, its meaning fixed for him by a supposed "jurisprudence of original intent," almost as though Steven Spielberg could transport Alexander Hamilton and James Madison to Ted Koppel's *Nightline* to tell us how they would approach electronic broadcasting or surrogate motherhood. According to this jurisprudence, the more liberal decisions of the Warren era and the Burger era represent illicit lawmaking rather than legitimate interpretation. The 1787 Constitution, according to Mr. Meese, expressed the people's consent to judicial intervention in defense of certain specified rights—and no others. It turns out that the rights Mr. Meese's Constitution empowers courts to protect from the masses (and from politically energized minorities) are largely the rights of the haves against the have-nots. They are largely the rights of the propertied classes—a happy coincidence for the Administration's political allies. In fact, it turns out that some of these apostles of judicial "restraint," at least in the case of recent circuit court nominees, like Professor Bernard Siegan of San Diego, are poised to hold the New Deal, and most social welfare legislation, unconstitutional—in the name of strict construction.

The opposite vision was stated most starkly by Supreme Court Justice Thurgood Marshall, speaking to a group of lawyers meeting in Hawaii earlier this month. Justice Marshall decried the original Constitution as defective. He denounced its framers as more bigoted than visionary. He stressed their willingness to preserve and protect slavery while professing to believe in freedom and equality. Only the Civil War, the Justice observed, ended that obscenity. For Justice Marshall, and I quote him, "The Union survived the Civil War, the Constitution did not."

Now, there is no way both Meese and Marshall can be right. But there is a way that both can be wrong. The "Meesianic" Constitution was, in fact, incomplete. It was proclaimed by "We the People," but "the people" who were the "We" in its Preamble tragically excluded blacks and women, and those who were without wealth or property. To celebrate that Constitution, according to its original intent, without acknowledging how much it left out—how far it had to evolve—is to ignore what may be the greatest achievement of the Founding Generation. That achievement was the legacy of a living Constitution—not only a Constitution capable of change, but a Constitution containing the tools for its own future development in the amendment provision of article V and in the judicial power of article III. And it contains not only the tools for its future development, but the seeds of its own future growth, in the form of a vision—a still imperfect vision—of a "more perfect Union" than the framers' own compromises had yet achieved. So Mr. Meese's Constitution is not the real Constitution.

But the Constitution of Thurgood Marshall is also incomplete. It denies its own roots—and its own still unresolved contradictions—in the process of professing its progressive character. To celebrate the Civil War amendments without acknowledging the basic framework of carefully separated and divided powers into which those amendments fit is to overlook the 18th-century institutional structures which alone made it possible for Congress, in the late 19th century and again after the mid-20th, to implement the amendments' guarantees. To disparage the work of 1787 is to overlook those institutional structures that made it possible for the Supreme Court of the United States, from the 1950's to the 1970's, after a century of national blindness, both to see, and to make the country face, what had to be done to redeem the fourteenth amendment's promise. To downplay the 1787 miracle at Philadelphia is to forget the institutional structures that made it possible for modern presidents like Dwight Eisenhower and John Fitzgerald Kennedy to breathe life into provisions that would otherwise have sounded marvelous but signified nothing—what Justice Jackson once called "a teasing illusion, like a munificent bequest in a pauper's will."

Keeping the Constitution's spirit alive thus means more than either celebrating its creation or lamenting its limitations. It means joining the enterprise of elaborating and extending its reach. That is the enterprise that I want to urge you to join as you leave this hall—and this university. But you must know that this enterprise has its adversaries. I urge you to identify those adversaries—and to do battle with them throughout your professional lives.

Those adversaries include many who say that they revere the Constitution but in fact give it a cramped and a narrow reading, a reading deeply inconsistent with its character as a flexible charter, deliberately drafted in broad strokes so that it might adapt without requiring too many abrupt and explicit amendments as society changes.

Those adversaries include many who would deploy the Constitution to remove government once again from the corporate boardroom and give government license to police every private bedroom in the land—as the Supreme Court decision about sodomy last summer authorized—all on the theory that love (but not greed) is the public's business, and that the framers were more worried about protecting the accumulation of property than about preserving space for human intimacy.

Those adversaries include many who are either ignorant of, or desperately eager to obscure, the Constitution's most basic premise—the premise that the laws bind all of government, including Generals and Lieutenant Colonels and, yes, even Presidents who genuinely see themselves, truly and patriotically, as "outside the Beltway," Presidents who think that Acts of Congress do not apply to the Oval Office when it orchestrates private and foreign efforts to circumvent the law.

Nothing could be more hostile to the spirit of constitutionalism than this sort of shadowy evasion—this effort to find paths, hidden in darkness, that are exempt from the light and the reach of legal and constitutional constraints.

For most of the Constitution's story, throughout our history, is a story of struggle to live by the Constitution's light—to extend its writ, making rights available to groups that had once been excluded, and making responsibilities attach to individuals who had once been exempted.

In this fundamental sense, the real framers of our Constitution were not only the propertied, white gentlemen who met in Philadelphia, but the many more—women and men, poor and rich, black, white, brown, and yellow—who marched and bled, who sang and rode buses and sat in and sometimes died, to make freedom ring.

Their song did not take all of its lyrics from the Constitution's literal text. How could it? Even the text itself proclaims its own incomplete, unfinished character. The ninth amendment expressly commands that the failure of the framers to spell out certain rights in so many words may not be used to justify the authoritarian conclusion that no such rights exist—the conclusion that government may enter every crevice of our private lives, and use every imaginable private device to get around the law, unless it was nailed shut by an explicit clause in the Constitution. Reducing the Constitution to a collection of explicit incantations, the way some would have us do, trivializes it in a way that is false to its most basic purposes.

There is a striking parallel between that kind of trivialization and some of what the would-be celebrants of the Bicentennial seem to have in mind. It is hard to be sure, but I suspect that the framers would have been appalled by the idea that the way to honor the Constitution they left us would be to carve it up into little pieces while forgetting its overarching purposes or to hand out 50 million tiny copies of the Constitution's text, like so many holy cards, as the Bicentennial Commission proposed not long ago. Constitutional literacy will not be achieved by sticking the text of the Bill of Rights onto every fast-food placemat, or by stuffing miniature copies of the document inside cereal boxes. Just imagine: "Equal Protection Clause Diet Cola," or "Necessary and Proper Clause Measuring Spoons!" The Saturday morning cartoons already feature Bugs Bunny and Elmer Fudd holding forth on bits and pieces of the Constitution. Squeezing more such pabulum between commercials for cornflakes and Go-Bots would not add much light to the subject. And yet a lot more light is needed.

Not long ago, the Hearst Corporation published a survey of the American public's knowledge of the Constitution. The findings were not very encouraging. Consider a few of the highlights:

> 45% of the people surveyed believe that the U.S. Constitution embodies the Marxist maxim, "From each according to his ability, to each according to his need."
>
> 49% of the American people believe that the President may suspend the Constitution whenever he declares a national emergency.
>
> 515 believe the Constitution does not permit a citizen to preach revolution—that, in a nation born of revolution.

Those are alarming numbers in a country whose Constitution depends on a fully informed citizenry. A century ago, James Russell Lowell warned that too many people had come to see the Constitution as a giant "machine that would go of itself." Twenty years later, Woodrow Wilson recognized that the Constitution is not a machine at all but, in his words, a "living thing."

What he did not add was that it is a very peculiar living thing. It has no body, no mind, no moving parts or organs or spirit, apart from the minds and bodies and spirits of the people themselves—people whose constant vigilance is the lifeblood of constitutional survival.

To keep the Constitution's promise, it is crucial that the people insist on compliance. If the people elect and retain leaders whose fidelity to the Constitution is a matter of convenient rhetoric—a fickle, sometime thing—leaders who praise the Constitution but scuttle it when it displeases them or when they believe they can get away with it—then it is the people, and not the Constitution, that must be held to account for what has gone awry.

When Presidents, or their aides, assume that they are above the law, then it is a cop-out to ask only: "What did the President know and when did he know it?" or even, "What did the President forget and when did he forget it?" All of us, Republicans and Democrats alike, must also ask: What have the people—all of us—forgotten about the requirements of genuine executive leadership and accountability in a constitutional democracy? We talk glibly about how the President must be held responsible for the actions of his subordinates. But we tend to forget that the President is our subordinate. We select him; he works for us; if we choose Presidents who are terrific at making us feel good, and at helping us to avoid facing hard realities, the ultimate responsibility for evading the Constitution is not theirs, but ours. "We have met the enemy," Pogo once said, "and they is us."

That is the most fundamental reason that we must not be content to celebrate the Constitution, or even to cerebrate it and study its meaning on this Bicentennial: We must decide to live it. To do no more than praise it is, in the end, to bury it.

I think back again to that *Mayflower* cartoon with which I opened these remarks. Why do we venerate that great ship? I think it is less because of the vessel it was than because of the voyage it began. And for those who would parade around the Constitution while turning back the clock of constitutional progress, the Constitution is like her naval namesake, the S.S. *Constitution*, now safely berthed in Boston Harbor, which I flew over yesterday—a curiosity for tourists, an obsolete and empty vessel good only for veneration.

But the Constitution of the United States is much more than that. It is a repository of memory and a call to progress. And, what is most important, the two are deeply linked. Justice Brennan was right when he reminded the narrow majority, in last month's decision about racial discrimination in the administration of the death penalty, that we ignore the evils of our own history at our peril: "[F]or," Justice Brennan said, "we remain imprisoned by the past as long as we deny its influence on the present."

I would add only this: We remain imprisoned by the past as long as we worship or revere it while ignoring its deepest lessons for our future. At a gathering of some 2,000 historians in Philadelphia last month, the focus was on the Constitution—but less on its origins than on the long line of dissenters and rebels who helped shape its development. Pete Seeger sang to the historians about working-class women and men. Son Thomas, from the Mississippi Delta, sang the blues—the music first of black dissent, then of power within despair, then of universal, undying hope.

What shall we say to those who come to praise the Constitution but would truly bury its redemptive message? Perhaps we should tell them to listen close. Maybe they, too, will hear the Bicentennial Blues.

## Essays from *Proceedings of the American Philosophical Society* 1987

275 YEARS AT THE AMERICAN PHILOSOPHICAL SOCIETY

# *The Dr. Richard A. F. Penrose Memorial Lecture: Remarks on the Constitutional Celebration*

**LORD SCARMAN**

*A Lord of Appeal*

I like the title which the Society suggested to me for my Penrose Memorial Lecture. There is about it an informality and lack of pomp and circumstance that would have delighted an erstwhile member of the Society, Thomas Jefferson. All I can hope is that what I have to say will prove to be what he would have wanted if he ever could have been persuaded to deliver a lecture—a contribution without frills to "useful knowledge." My remarks will fall into three sections, each of which, though they will overlap, will have a distinct theme:

I. The fundamental difference between the U.S. and the British constitutions:
II. The distinctive American contributions to constitution-making
III. Is the British constitution on the move?

But before I get down to my task, let me invite you to include in your constitutional celebration three men: Jefferson, Madison, and Alexander Hamilton; one system of jurisprudence, the common law; and an institution, the American Philosophical Society. Jefferson, of course, did not participate in the work of the Philadelphia Convention: Hamilton and Madison did, and are entitled to much of the credit for the draft constitution that emerged. Madison was certainly inspired by Jeffersonian ideas. Though Hamilton would never have admitted that he could derive inspiration from Jefferson, he shared with Jefferson a belief in a strong executive and used his great influence to ensure that the new federal state would not suffer from the executive weakness, which nearly lost the Confederation the War of Independence. And all three men were prepared to base the constitution on the common law. I suppose we must thank Madison in particular for building into the draft the very special combination of the ideas of the age of enlightenment with the principles of the common law.

I would celebrate the Society not only for its longevity but because it has, to the surprise of some, included legal knowledge as a legitimate subject in its promotion of useful knowledge. The Society has given place, but not supremacy, to law as a subject. This itself is Jeffersonian; he never was a man to put law above its proper station in human affairs. He saw law as a means to an end. He thought it self-evident that the rule of law itself has to be justified: and the American justification is that it must be founded on certain unalienable rights, among them life, liberty, and the pursuit of happiness. The Society is to be saluted for widening this noble vision so that it includes the promotion of knowledge and the development of the arts and sciences. Happiness is more than food and shelter: It is the chance to live a civilized life.

## I. THE ANGLO-AMERICAN DIFFERENCE

The American constitution embodied in a legal structure what was a political act, the Declaration of Independence. There is no comparable sequence in British history. Over the years the formalities of the British constitution have lost touch with the reality of power. The formal structure of the British constitution is no more than a dignified façade behind which there operates a political process. The constitutional protection of the rights and freedoms of an American citizen is legal in character and enforceable in the courts against the executive and the legislature. Though law plays an important role in protecting the rights of the British people, the ultimate constitutional protection of British rights and freedoms is political: this is because there is no legal limit to the legislative sovereignty of Parliament other than the purely formal requirement of the monarch's assent: the enacting words are:

> "Le roi le veult"—significantly in old, if not Norman, French.

The British experience of reliance upon the political process has, however, during this century and particularly in the years since 1945, exposed certain weaknesses that have disturbed public opinion. I shall discuss in my third section the question that is now being asked in Britain: Should we introduce legal safeguards into our constitution to supplement the protection provided by Parliament? Many of us—let me say at once I am one of them—believe that we must and that we will.

The British constitution is, of course, no child of revolution: As a matter of history, its legitimacy is not in doubt. Questions can be raised—though never in Philadelphia—about the legitimacy of the American constitution: And in drafting the Declaration of Independence Jefferson sought to establish the legitimacy of a constitution brought into existence by revolution. He succeeded: And his success revolutionized the political philosophy of the Western world. He refuted any suggestion that people under oppression imposed by a lawfully established government had no right to throw off the government. He found the right self-evident, which he explained as meaning that it was justified by "laws of nature and of nature's God." This justification was not original. The Roman jurists and the Greek philosophers had recognized a law variously called "jus naturale," "jus gentium." The political philosophers of eighteenth-century Europe had explored the idea of a people's right of revolution against tyranny. They had evolved the concepts of sovereign power vested in the people and of the social contract as the legitimate foundation of the rights and duties of government. Jefferson's conclusion enshrined in the Declaration of Independence was not, therefore, an original concept: What was new was that a people—the people of America—embodied the concept in action and built a working constitution based on the natural rights of man—rights which by their very nature set limits upon the powers of government.

The purpose of the Declaration and the Constitution which followed was, however, not generalist in character, nor was it a total break with the past. In these respects the two instruments differed radically from their French contemporaries, the "Declaration des Droits de l'Homme" and the new revolutionary republic. This was not surprising. A revolution engineered by common lawyers is no "trahison des clercs," let alone a rout of established society by a maddened proletariat. Common lawyers are trained to take their cases not a whit beyond what is needed to win. The American Revolution's purpose was to rid the people of the despotic power of the King of Great Britain, but not to reject the principles of law by which the British people lived. When, therefore, in 1787 the independent states of America accepted their new constitution, they retained the common law. They had, of course, a practical problem (which loomed large in Hamilton's thinking, and later in that of the Federalists): How does one fill the vacuum created by the rejection of the King? The answer of the Philadelphia Convention was a constitutional contract established by and for the people specifying and limiting the powers of government. But the Convention knew that within its sphere each arm of government must be strong, independent of the others but ultimately answerable not to a governor, be it one man or an assembly, but to the people themselves. The most memorable departure from the British tradition (other than the rejection of monarchical sovereignty) was the enhanced constitutional role given to the judicial power. The Convention created a structure in which a president with great but defined powers exercised the executive power; in which an elected Congress exercised the legislative power within the limits and subject to the restraints set by the Constitution; and in which a judicial power, though it could not initiate action, was to be the final arbiter in all cases in law and equity arising under the Constitution. The separation of powers as translated into the Constitution carried with it definitions and limitations of power which aggrieved citizens and others, including the individual States of the Union, could enforce by bringing a case to court. Here was a social contract indeed, and one that safeguarded the rights of the people as its major party and the ultimate beneficiary.

But there was more to the Constitution than a marriage of convenience between the common law and the political theories of the age of enlightenment. I refer to the federal principle. By it the people of America established a sovereign union of independent states—on the face of it a logical impossibility.

At a later stage, I shall set out some reasons for believing that the federal principle was a truly original American idea. For the moment, I content myself with selecting what I would suggest are the four most important contributions to be found in the Constitution to the development of civilization. I suggest that they are the federal principle, the defining of presidential and congressional power without emasculating either, the Bill of Rights, and the establishment of the judicial watchdog to guard the Constitution.

These four features, by emphasizing the contractual nature of the Constitution, enabled the American people to establish a sovereign union of free peoples by peaceful expansion over a continent stretching from the Atlantic to the Pacific. And the work was done when communications depended upon the horse, such rivers as nature provided, and the sailing ship. Remarkable, indeed!

The British have been inhibited, at home if not overseas, from a similar constitutional development by the formalities of power which their unbroken history has invested with the magical character of holy writ. The Queen, in theory, exercises sovereign power with the advice and consent of Parliament. As everyone knows, this is a fiction. Parliament is sovereign. And even this, though true, does not reflect where power really resides. Parliament has two houses: One of them has, save for a single critically important exception, legislative sovereignty—the House of Commons. And the same House can, by a majority vote, force the resignation of a government.

The House of Lords, by contrast, has today very limited powers. It can impose delay upon the passing of legislation: It has a power, which it uses to good effect, of reviewing and amending legislation proposed by the Commons: and it has the right to propose legislation (its members frequently introduce Bills and the Government itself frequently chooses to introduce legislation in the House). But it cannot stop a determined House of Commons. It is this unstoppable power of the Commons which ensures that a government which in the Commons commands a majority, however small or irresponsible, can get its way. It led Lord Hailsham to echo Jefferson by speaking of the danger in the United Kingdom of an elected dictatorship. In his "Notes on the State of Virginia" Jefferson spoke of the danger of concentrating all the power of government in the same hands: the danger, he said, of an "elective despotism."[1] That danger is built into the effective, the real British constitution. There is only one escape: And that is difficult and insecure. The House of Commons cannot prolong the life of a Parliament without the consent of the House of Lords: That is to say, it cannot enact against the opposition of the Lords the postponement of a general election beyond the period set by law of 5 years from the last general election. A valuable safeguard, but difficult to reconcile within democratic principles. A House, unelected, part hereditary, part appointed, its members holding their places for life, is relied upon as the ultimate constitutional guarantee of the people's right to choose their government. But the system works. Indeed the House of Lords currently enjoys a greater respect than the elected House: Its sense of responsibility and the thoughtfulness of its debates, though not very exciting, are cherished by the people.

Put briefly, there are no legal limits upon the sovereign power of the Commons, save that the House cannot extend its life beyond the period set by law save with the assent of the Lords. But even the sovereign power of the Commons is exercised not so much by its members as by the government of the day. Thanks to the party system, power is exercised by the party that commands a majority in the Commons. The power of Parliament has become largely a power available to the government of the day, though the Commons

---

[1]Notes, Ford III pp. 223–24.

by withdrawing support can defeat the government and force an election. For most of the time, therefore, the party with a majority is uninhibited by any constitutional restraints upon its power. And the courts have no restraining power. They are, of course, independent and impartial: Their decisions bind litigants, but they are bound to obey the legislative will of Parliament. Finally, even the one safeguard that the Commons needs the assent of the Lords to extend their period in office can itself be abolished by legislation which could be passed overriding the requirement of the Lords' assent.

I have emphasized the weakness of the legal safeguards of the British constitution to point the contrast with the American Constitution. But this weakness does not cause in practice anything like the trouble that it could evoke in theory. Why? Because the political safeguards, though not legally enforceable, are strong. They are democratic. The British constitution, being unwritten, cannot be pinned down: It is not a matter of words in a statute to be interpreted by the courts but a way of life of the whole people. It is possible, and true, to say, of the British Constitution that it is as intangible and yet as pervasive as air: It is the invisible but vital atmosphere in which the country operates. One begins with the common law. This has been created by centuries of judicial decision and remains the law of the land as determined by the judges unless and until abrogated or modified by Act of Parliament. The political process, operated by Parliament and the government, is answerable to the people and is a combination that is for most of the time dominated by the government. Nevertheless the legislature and the executive follow practices and conventions that represent Parliament's self-imposed restraints upon what it may properly do or not do. In the result the liberty of the subject is as a matter of policy left to the judges to protect. For example, Parliament would not, save in time of national emergency, suspend habeas corpus, allow imprisonment without trial, suppress free speech, or censor the press. But, if Parliament does legislate in such matters, the judges have to accept it: Witness the notorious section 2 of the Official Secrets Act, which is used to inhibit freedom of information on matters which the government does not wish to be made known. Nevertheless, Parliament does provide an effective political protection of the liberties of our people. And the policies of Parliament based on universal suffrage are truly democratic. Doubts, however, are arising as to whether this protection ought not now to be supplemented by constitutional safeguards enforceable by legal process in the courts—a question to which I shall return in the last section of my address. It may be that we shall seek to support political process by a legal process in an endeavor to protect our people against the misuse of power.

## II. THE DISTINCTIVE AMERICAN CONTRIBUTIONS TO CONSTITUTION-MAKING

I constantly remind myself that the Constitution of 1787 and the ten amendments of 1791 were common law documents. They were drafted by common lawyers and each proceeds upon the basis of common law principles. Let me give a few illustrations.

First. Article I section (9)(1)(2) of the Constitution:

> The privilege of the writ of habeas corpus shall not be suspended, unless when in cases of rebellion or invasion the public safety may require it.

Secondly. Article III section 2(1) of the Constitution:

> The judicial power shall extend to all cases, in law and equity, arising under this Constitution.

Thirdly, from the Bill of Rights:

The First Amendment itself, which needs no quotation; and the Seventh Amendment *preserving* the right of trial by jury in suits at common law. The Constitution and the Bill of Rights assume a substratum of common law.

The common law character of the Constitution is trite stuff for members of the Society: But it is not fully understood, let alone its implications appreciated, in my country. In our legitimate reverence for the judge-made common law and in our undoubted affection for our unwritten constitution, we too easily assume that each needs the other to survive. This is not true. The United States have by what they have done exposed the fallacy of the assumption. The common law has thrived and developed in the hands of American judges interpreting and enforcing a written constitution. In a very real sense the Constitution magnifies and strengthens the common law. To take two examples, freedom of the press and due process, are common law principles that enjoy the protection of the Constitution. Both principles exist in the U.K., where, however, their constitutional protection is in the political process. If Parliament should choose to restrict, suspend, or deny either of them, the courts could not prevent or challenge what was happening. The truth is that the American Constitution provides the common law with a protection that it lacks in Britain.

The second feature to which I would draw attention is the federal principle. It is a simple enough concept, though its embodiment in a working constitution presents complex problems. It is really a governmental mechanism that the U.S.A. has elevated into a principle. Napoleon, a contemporary you will remember of the U.S.A. and of the American Philosophical Society, might himself have federated Europe, had the British allowed him the time to do so. But, if he had it would have been an imposition, it would have borne no resemblance to the American model, a federation of free states and peoples. The American concept of federation was based on the social contract: Federation was seen as a partnership exercising sovereign power for the benefit of its members who retain their independence while they accept the obligations of partnership. And the American vision penetrated beyond the member states of the Union to the people of those states. The federal principle became a direct channel of power and responsibility between the people and the government of the Union notwithstanding the presence in the Union of the independent member states. This was genius. The first words of the Preamble to the Constitution sum it all up:

> We, the people of the United States . . . do ordain and establish this Constitution for the United States of America.

The direct federal link between the people and the Union was not allowed to destroy the states. The concept of partnership (itself, as I have argued, the creature of the social contract) enabled the states to retain their independent existence while agreeing to the restrictions needed "in order to form a more perfect union."

The concept of a federation of free and independent states, in which the people as well as the states were partners and the intended beneficiaries, was American. Some might say that the seed was sown in the Fundamental Orders of 1639. It was assuredly a fine way of achieving Jefferson's vision of a continental America: And I believe that this vision was made possible and practical by the Constitution.

Jefferson and others concerned with laying the foundations of the American continental union of peoples never forgot that to the north, the west, and the south of the Atlantic states there stretched a largely unexplored land mass. True, the French and the Spaniards had made some penetration in the south and southwest; and the British were a presence in Canada. But in the struggle for expansion into the land mass of America, the U.S.A. had a head start: The Union was an American power with its base and headquarters in America.

After their experience as colonists subject to imperial power, the founding fathers of the Union were determined to expand into the continent not by force of arms but peaceably and with the assent of the people who had settled there. They used the federal idea to this end. The idea was implicit in the Northwest Ordinance of 1787, which we surely should be celebrating this year as fervently as the Constitution itself. The Ordinance was an enduring achievement of the Confederation. It contained two provisions of fundamental importance. Article 6 prohibited slavery in the Northwest territory. Article 5 provided a right to be vested in states to be formed "to be admitted into the Congress of the United States on an equal footing with the original states in all respects whatever." The one condition was that the new states must be republics. How different the progress of the U.S.A. and the North American continent from the progress of the Roman or the British Empire! Not a trace of colonialism: No subjection of free men to the will of an emperor: a partnership, not an empire. There were only two flaws—the protection of the Constitution was only very tardily extended to Red Indians, and to slaves. But that it should be so extended was implicit in the Northwest Ordinance.

By your own development of the federal concept you of the U.S.A. have taught a lesson to the civilized world. Sovereign power can be diminished to serve the public good without losing its strength, and without destroying local or regional independence. A sovereign state can serve the interests of all without overwhelming the independence of its constituent parts: and the whole complex edifice can be answerable directly to a free people whose government it is, and at the same time can provide strong government at home and abroad.

I select one other feature of the Constitution for special mention—the constitutional role which it gives to the judicial power. In Britain the courts were in the beginning an emanation of royal power: Today they are the creatures of the statute law enacted by Parliament. An Act of Parliament can sweep them away and substitute, if Parliament should so choose, some other method of adjudication. Parliament can and frequently does restrict or extend their jurisdiction, create new tribunals, alter the appellate process, and change their procedures. Article III of the American Constitution, however, gives a constitutional status and guarantee of continued existence and independent power to the Supreme Court, the judges of which are appointed by the president by and with the advice and consent of the Senate and hold office during good behavior. Some have held that they can be removed from office only on impeachment, though I have always doubted this construction of the Constitution. Be that as it may, their tenure of office is protected by the Constitution as is the Supreme Court itself.

True to the doctrine of separation of powers, the Constitution effectually establishes a separate and independent judicial power. But it says little, or nothing explicit, about the extent of the judicial power. Article III section 2(1) clearly envisages the power extending to controversies to which the U.S. shall be a party and to controversies between two or more states: But does the Constitution envisage judicial review of executive decisions? And, if so, how far can judicial review be taken? And does it envisage judicial review of the legislative acts of Congress? The answer to the first question was answered by the decisions of Marshall's Supreme Court analyzing the necessary implications of the Constitution. But I find nothing in the Constitution compelling the Supreme Court to go as far as Marshall C. J. went in *Marbury v. Madison*[2] when, speaking obiter (for it was not necessary to the court's decision), he asserted the power of the Supreme Court to strike down legislation considered by the court to be unconstitutional. Jefferson, a strict constitutionalist, never liked this decision. But there is nothing in the Constitution expressly denying such a power. And by now history has opted in favor of Marshall's view as to the extent of the judicial power of the Union. The Supreme Court enjoys, therefore, the power to strike down unconstitutional acts of the Congress as well as abuse of executive power by the government. Thus the separation of powers was carried by judicial interpretation of the Constitution to its logical conclusion, the exercise of each power being limited by definition but in its sphere subject only to the Constitution.

The contrast with Britain is stark. Parliament is sovereign: The executive survives only with its assent: And the judges cannot question the validity of Acts of Parliament.

## III. IS THE BRITISH CONSTITUTION ON THE MOVE?

Constitutional change may, however, be on its way in Britain. There are indications, faint but genuine, of a constitutional law (by which I mean a constitution legally enforceable) looming over a not too distant horizon. The existing void is the fault—if lack of interest be a fault—of an uncaring legal profession, uncaring, I hasten to add, until the recent developments of which I propose to give you an outline. English common lawyers have accepted for the last 300 years (we celebrate the tercentenary of our so-called Bill of Rights in either 1988 or 1989: we do not really know that date and it is not really a Bill of Rights) that constitutional law is the business of Parliament, not the

[2] Cranch (5 U.S.) 137 (1803).

courts. The common law has been seen as a system of criminal justice and, in its civil aspect, as a system of distributive justice. Some great figures of our law, notably Bacon, Coke, and Blackstone, have had a wider vision: but they were exceptional. Coke's assertion in *Bonham's*[3] case that the courts can declare void an unreasonable and unjust Act of Parliament was deprived of effect and remaindered to the history books by the Act of Settlement and Bill of Rights in 1688/89. Today, however, a change of attitude is discernible. It began shortly after the end of the 1939–45 war. The war created a new social situation, the demand for a welfare state. It also left in the hearts and minds of the people of Europe a determination never to allow a recurrence of the horrors perpetrated by Nazi Germany. How could a highly civilized people, leaders in European culture and thought, fall into the hands of a cruel, bigoted, and tyrannical government? How came it that such a great people tolerated what was done in their name? If this could happen in Germany, were any of us safe in our own country? Safeguards had to be built while memories were fresh. This was the birth in Europe of the human rights movement. How were human rights to be protected against infringement by our own governments?

In Britain we met the social demand by enacting the welfare state. We answered the human rights question by joining with other like-minded European states to form the Council of Europe.

## The Welfare State

Very briefly, we in Britain established by statute a complex of social benefits to be made available by the state to those in need. The benefits were rights in such fields as unemployment, industrial injury, health, education, old age, pensions, and poverty. If the state should fail to meet a person's entitlement, he could have resort to an appropriate tribunal with the ultimate sanction of judicial review by the High Court.

## The Human Rights Question

The answer to this question has proved infinitely more difficult for us. Our difficulties, not felt by other members of the Council of Europe, are peculiar to the United Kingdom: They arise from the void in our constitutional law.

[3]Coke, 8 Co. Rep. 1142.

The Council of Europe—not to be confused with the E.E.C.—was established with the object of securing within Europe the purposes and principles of the United Nations. The Council's first and major task, successfully completed by 1950, was to prepare the European Convention of Human Rights and Fundamental Freedoms based on the 1948 United Nations' Declaration of Human Rights. The United Kingdom signed and in 1953 ratified the Convention, thereby accepting the obligation in international law to secure to all persons within its jurisdiction the rights and freedoms guaranteed by the Convention. The Convention broke new ground by establishing a Commission and a Court—the European Commission and the European Court of Human Rights sitting in Strasbourg—to whom persons or states can have resort if a member state infringes any of the rights and freedoms guaranteed by the Convention. However, individuals can petition Strasbourg only if the member state has allowed the right of petition to the Commission and accepted the compulsory jurisdiction of the Court. Britain has allowed the right of petition and has accepted the compulsory jurisdiction of the Court.

The rights and freedoms guaranteed by the Convention are the political and civil rights, with one or two important additions (notably an extended right of privacy), which are recognized and protected by the common law. Accordingly, the Convention covers much of the ground covered by the American Bill of Rights.

Had the U.S.A., by its president with the advice and consent of the Senate, entered into a treaty comparable with the European Convention, that fact would have sufficed to have incorporated the Convention into U.S.A. law and would have given the judicial power of the U.S. jurisdiction to deal with infringements of the Convention arising in the U.S. And this is the position with almost all the signatory states of the Convention: But not so in Britain. International treaties form no part of our internal law unless expressly incorporated by statute, and Parliament has not so enacted.

The consequence of this anomaly is that there has been an increasing number of petitions to the European Commission of Human Rights in Strasbourg alleging infringements by Britain of the Convention for which our courts can provide no remedy. Britain has had to face the embarrassment of a number of these petitions resulting in findings by the European Court of Human Rights that British law has failed to provide a remedy for an infringement of a human right, which, by accepting the Convention, Britain had undertaken to guarantee. True, the British government acts, after the event of a finding against it, to compensate the petitioner and to amend the law. But the words "after the event" conceal major injustice. For the citizen will have had to fight his way to Strasbourg after failing to get a remedy from the courts or the administration at home. This passage to Strasbourg is slow, tortuous, uncertain, and expensive. If he gets a result from the European Court of Human Rights within 5 years of the wrong done to him, he may count himself fortunate.

And so in Britain the question is being asked: Why not shorten and cheapen the citizen's redress by incorporating the European Convention into British law, thereby enabling our national courts to enforce the Convention against our own government, which, of course, has accepted its obligations? Of course, this could only be achieved by legislation. If it were done, the effect would be to establish the European Convention as a Bill of Rights operative in our internal law and enforceable in the courts of the land. But even so a Bill of Rights so enacted could at any time be amended or repealed by Parliament: It would not have the guarantee of being part of a written constitution protected by the judicial power.

The House of Lords has responded to the challenge. Twice in the last few years it has passed through all its stages a Bill which, if enacted, would have incorporated the Convention into British law. On each occasion the House of Commons has by procedural maneuvers blocked the passage of the Bill through that House. But there is some progress. In February of this year 94 members of the House of Commons voted in favor of giving the Bill a second reading. It was defeated on a point of procedure.

In summary, some of us have concluded that the United Kingdom must adopt a written constitution based on separation of powers and providing the citizen with greater constitutional protection against abuse of power. The judicial power would be assigned the role of protecting the citizen against abuse of state power. In Britain the judges have already adopted, without hindrance from Parliament, a higher profile in developing judicial review of the administrative decisions of the executive in the area of the welfare state. The European Convention has exposed weaknesses in our law's protection of human rights so that pressure is building for a Bill of Rights enforceable like the statutes of the welfare state in British courts.

We are still a long way from a constitution comparable with that of the U.S.A. But if the United Kingdom should accept, as I believe it will, a federal structure devolving to the regions of England, Scotland, Wales, and Northern Ireland, the unity of the Kingdom and the need for equal rights under the law in all its regions would require a written constitution and judicial protection of the rights guaranteed to the citizen by that constitution.

For these reasons I am proud to be invited to speak to you in celebration of the American Constitution. My countrymen will, I believe, find in the American Constitution much to help them in devising a constitution suitable for their complex needs. As we go into the twenty-first century, we have to adapt our constitution to the social, economic, and political needs of a multiracial society. Democracy has always meant rule by the majority tempered by respect for the interests of minorities. There are now many minorities in our society for whom the political process provides at best an uncertain protection. We need strong government but within limits set by a constitutional law: And we need a fundamental law of human rights enforceable by the judicial power. America has shown the world how it can be done. For that reason I feel deeply honored by your invitation to salute you in Philadelphia in 1987.

## EPILOGUE

I cannot resist the temptation, however, to twist the tail of the animal I so much admire. What business had Madison, Hamilton, and their colleagues in the Convention, to draft a constitution? Did not Congress call a Convention in Philadelphia solely to revise the Articles of Confederation in the interests of "the trade and commerce of the United States"? Certainly that was Hamilton's recommendation. Trade and commerce have much to answer for. On American soil they can make constitutions.

# Symposium on the United States Constitution

# *The Miracle at Philadelphia*


## ARLIN ADAMS

*Judge, United States Court of Appeals, Retired*


In approximately five months, the nation will mark the 200th anniversary of the signing of the Constitution. It was here in Philadelphia, on 17 September 1787, that the document was affirmed by 39 delegates from the thirteen states of the Confederation.

During the past 200 years, we have emerged from a small, loose confederation of states into a strong federal union, composed of individual sovereign states.

What happened from May to September in 1787 is often referred to as the "Miracle at Philadelphia." It is important to recall the experience of the 13 states under the Articles of Confederation and the Continental Congress, which were created by them. For it was incidents occurring between 1776 and 1786 which were the moving force behind the drafting of the Constitution.

The Articles of Confederation provided for a perpetual union or as the Articles put it, a "firm league of friendship" among the states. Unfortunately, the Continental Congress could not levy taxes, enlist troops, or regulate interstate or foreign commerce. It could not force any state into compliance and it could not enforce its authority on any individual. The major accomplishment under the Articles was the adoption of the Ordinance of 1787 for the governance and disposition of the Northwest Territory. The colonies went through the revolution to be free of British rule, but at the same time they wanted to regain the sovereign status that each had with the other colonies before the war. After the revolution, although there was some sense of loyalty to the new nation, there was a far greater attachment by the citizens to each individual state.

Because the Continental Congress had little power, it provided no substantial foundation on which to build a new nation. By 1788, the prestige of the Continental Congress was so low that some states no longer bothered to send representatives to its meetings. Although the Treaty of Paris of 1783, in which we theoretically resolved our differences with England, was achieved by the Continental Congress, it was really more the accomplishment of a single person, the then Secretary for Foreign Affairs, John Jay.

England recognized the ineffectiveness of the new confederation and took advantage of it. For example, it declined to trade with its former colonies. It knew that Americans had no other nation to trade with except Britain, and that the Continental Congress had no way of retaliating if the British refused to send goods to this country. Not only was our commerce threatened by Britain, but Britain refused to withdraw its troops from the frontier posts on American soil, and stirred the Indians against the new country.

Jay warned the Continental Congress that Americans must continue to be prepared for war, but the army had been disbanded and there was no means to raise a new one. Britain was arrogant and there was little that the Confederation could do about it.

For their part, the individual states refused to recognize their earlier debts to British creditors. There was no recognition by the states of the provision placed in the Treaty of Paris for protection of Tory property, and the states continued to confiscate this property in violation of the Paris Treaty. Indeed, there was no way to compel the states to honor any of the unpopular provisions of the Treaty.

Not only was our relationship with England cumbersome and inept, but we had considerable concern about free navigation on the Mississippi, a principal route to the sea. Spain closed the lower Mississippi to citizens of the new nation, and levied taxes and tariffs at New Orleans on all American products. It began to appear at that time that Spain and Britain were in a conspiracy to sever the western territories from the new union. Even France, America's wartime ally, showed little respect for the new confederation. And in the Mediterranean, the Barbary states displayed open contempt for the weak young nation.

Back home, there was a dispute among the eastern and southern states as to how the new lands of the west should be divided. The states' claims to western lands resulted in small-scale shooting wars and various plots. Ethan Allen, on behalf of Vermont, attempted to negotiate a separate treaty with Britain that would have made Vermont a province of Canada. Northern alliances and southern divisions began to form. As one historical account observed, there was diverse sectionalism everywhere.

To the Rev. Mr. Lathrop
from B. Franklin

WE, the People of the United States, in order to form a more perfect union, establish justice, insure domestic tranquility, provide for the common defence, promote the general welfare, and secure the blessings of liberty to ourselves and our posterity, do ordain and establish this Constitution for the United States of America.

ARTICLE I.

*Sect.* 1. ALL legislative powers herein granted shall be vested in a Congress of the United States, which shall consist of a Senate and House of Representatives.

*Sect.* 2. The House of Representatives shall be composed of members chosen every second year by the people of the several states, and the electors in each state shall have the qualifications requisite for electors of the most numerous branch of the state legislature.

No person shall be a representative who shall not have attained to the age of twenty-five years, and been seven years a citizen of the United States, and who shall not, when elected, be an inhabitant of that state in which he shall be chosen.

Representatives and direct taxes shall be apportioned among the several states which may be included within this Union, according to their respective numbers, which shall be determined by adding to the whole number of free persons, including those bound to service for a term of years, and excluding Indians not taxed, three-fifths of all other persons. The actual enumeration shall be made within three years after the first meeting of the Congress of the United States, and within every subsequent term of ten years, in such manner as they shall by law direct. The number of representatives shall not exceed one for every thirty thousand, but each state shall have at least one representative; and until such enumeration shall be made, the state of New-Hampshire shall be entitled to chuse three, Massachusetts eight, Rhode-Island and Providence Plantations one, Connecticut five, New-York six, New-Jersey four, Pennsylvania eight, Delaware one, Maryland six, Virginia ten, North-Carolina five, South-Carolina five, and Georgia three.

When vacancies happen in the representation from any state, the Executive authority thereof shall issue writs of election to fill such vacancies.

The House of Representatives shall chuse their Speaker and other officers; and shall have the sole power of impeachment.

*Sect.* 3. The Senate of the United States shall be composed of two senators from each state, chosen by the legislature thereof, for six years; and each senator shall have one vote.

Immediately after they shall be assembled in consequence of the first election, they shall be divided as equally as may be into three classes. The seats of the senators of the first class shall be vacated at the expiration of the second year, of the second class at the expiration of the fourth year, and of the third class at the expiration of the sixth year, so that one-third may be chosen every second year; and if vacancies happen by resignation, or otherwise, during the recess of the Legislature of any state, the Executive thereof may make temporary appointments until the next meeting of the Legislature, which shall then fill such vacancies.

No person shall be a senator who shall not have attained to the age of thirty years, and been nine years a citizen of the United States, and who shall not, when elected, be an inhabitant of that state for which he shall be chosen.

The Vice-President of the United States shall be President of the senate, but shall have no vote, unless they be equally divided.

The Senate shall chuse their other officers, and also a President pro tempore, in the absence of the Vice-President, or when he shall exercise the office of President of the United States.

The Senate shall have the sole power to try all impeachments. When sitting for that purpose, they shall be on oath or affirmation. When the President of the United States is tried, the Chief Justice shall preside: And no person shall be convicted without the concurrence of two-thirds of the members present.

Judgment in cases of impeachment shall not extend further than to removal from office, and disqualification to hold and enjoy any office of honor, trust or profit under the United States; but the party convicted shall nevertheless be liable and subject to indictment, trial, judgment and punishment, according to law.

*Sect.* 4. The times, places and manner of holding elections for senators and representatives, shall be prescribed in each state by the legislature thereof; but the Congress may at any time by law make or alter such regulations, except as to the places of chusing Senators.

The Congress shall assemble at least once in every year, and such meeting shall be on the first Monday in December, unless they shall by law appoint a different day.

*Sect.* 5. Each house shall be the judge of the elections, returns and qualifications of its own members, and a majority of each shall constitute a quorum to do business; but a smaller number may adjourn from day to day, and may be authorised to compel the attendance of absent members, in such manner, and under such penalties as each house may provide.

Each house may determine the rules of its proceedings, punish its members for disorderly behaviour, and, with the concurrence of two-thirds, expel a member.

Each house shall keep a journal of its proceedings, and from time to time publish the same, excepting such parts as may in their judgment require secrecy; and the yeas and nays of the members of either house on any question shall, at the desire of one-fifth of those present, be entered on the journal.

Neither house, during the session of Congress, shall, without the consent of the other, adjourn for more than three days, nor to any other place than that in which the two houses shall be sitting.

*Sect.* 6. The senators and representatives shall receive a compensation for their services, to be ascertained by law, and paid out of the treasury of the United States. They shall in all cases, except treason, felony and breach of the peace, be privileged from arrest during their attendance at the

**Benjamin Franklin's copy of the Constitution with marginal notes.**
**American Philosophical Society.**

Another fundamental problem was the question of finance. Congress had a debt of almost $40 million, not counting the debts of the several states. Robert Morris declared that, "talking to the states about money was like preaching to the dead." The Articles did not give the Continental Congress the power to tax. Trade among the new states was another problem. New Jersey was said to have levied duties on goods brought in through other states, and New York retaliated by assessing high fees on goods entering from Connecticut and New Jersey.

A national coining system was established in 1785, but few coins appeared until 1793. Seven of the 13 states resorted to paper money, but its value rapidly depreciated despite laws making it legal tender. Depression set in across the country. Mortgage foreclosures in Massachusetts were at an all-time high. Jails were jammed with debtors.

After Daniel Shay's rebellion in Massachusetts, where farm debtors marched against county court houses, Washington wrote to Madison on 5 November 1786, and said: "We are fast emerging to anarchy and confusion."

Washington invited commissioners from some of the states to meet and to attempt to adopt a uniform commercial system. It was Madison, however, who proposed that the states amend the Articles of Confederation to provide for some type of specific commercial regulation. Although five states sent delegates to the Annapolis convention in September 1786, none of the New England states was present. The Annapolis meeting recommended that delegates from all the states gather at Philadelphia in May of 1787 to make the changes "necessary to render the constitution of the federal government adequate to the needs of the union."

Fundamental to our modern-day understanding is that the drafters of the Constitution were attempting to create a bond of federalism for the American states in order to avoid domestic violence and the threat of foreign powers. To put it another way, the main purpose of the convention was "to form a more perfect union."

Today, almost two centuries after the drafting of that remarkable document, we are going to discuss a number of important aspects of it with four eminently qualified authorities.

# *Separation of Powers—Then and Now*


## NICHOLAS deB. KATZENBACH

*Partner, Riker, Danzig, Scherer, Hyland & Perretti*


When we think of Constitutional issues today we most often have in mind the individual rights and freedoms incorporated in the Amendments to it and not the structural provisions which compose the bulk of the Constitution itself and which, quite appropriately, occupied the bulk of the discussions in the summer of 1787. To constitute a government was, after all, the underlying purpose of the Convention.

It is little short of a miracle that the structure specified in our written Constitution has survived for two centuries with relatively few changes. Undoubtedly credit must go to those remarkable men who wrote it. And, I believe, an equal credit must go to the political genius of those who followed—who created institutions outside the Constitution itself that have enabled a political structure, awkward at best, to work reasonably well through the extraordinary changes of the last two hundred years. And principal among these has been the political party—an institution in great difficulty today and without which, I suggest, our Constitutional political structure will not work well, if, indeed, it will work at all.

Thus it is an appropriate time to look at our political structure, not merely to celebrate the wisdom of the Founding Fathers, but to reflect on the problems they sought to solve and on contemporary problems related in part to the structure they created, and in large part to the technology of modern society. I have in mind not the technology of weapons—important as that is—but simply the technology of communication, primarily television, because television has had and is having an enormous impact on our political institutions and the way our federal government works. To the extent television has destroyed political parties as the essential bridge linking the separate powers of Congress

Alexander Hamilton.

Engraving by William S. Leney. Courtesy of the Library Company of Philadelphia.

and the president, it is destroying our capacity to govern ourselves. Despite presidential and congressional rhetoric, we seem unable to confront and resolve such vitally important problems as budget deficits and trade imbalances. Everyone acknowledges the seriousness of the problem, everyone acknowledges that there are cures; but we cannot agree on any particular cure. No one blames this seeming paralysis on the Founding Fathers and the political structure they created. Nor do I—at least not in the sense that I want to suggest radical changes. But surely it is obvious that our separation of powers—the segmentation of legislative and executive powers—lies at the heart of our inability to act. And, for this reason, there are serious and knowledgeable people—both scholars and political leaders—who are asking if we can continue to afford the luxury of our unique political structure.

Our political concept of a strong legislature and a relatively weak executive was, of course, strongly influenced by the experience of the Revolution and the determination, perhaps even stronger in the country at large than in Philadelphia, not to have a potential George III. It was reinforced by those who had suspicions of the federal government itself, even though they recognized the need for some limited functions and for a chief executive. The Constitution clearly puts responsibility for determining national policy in the Congress, not the president.

What has permitted this cumbersome governmental structure to survive with relatively few constitutional changes has been our political creativity plus, of course, a civil war. I would single out the obvious: the creation of political parties; the Supreme Court's arrogation of the ultimate power to interpret the Constitution; and, a function of political parties, standing the Electoral College on its head by converting independent electors into automatons. By thus, in effect, having a president elected by the people (though not necessarily by a majority) this last development could be viewed as creating a more democratic national government. So, too, of course, could the direct election of Senators, and permitting women and former slaves to vote. But although less elitist than the Founding Fathers intended, the national government has remained more representative than democratic and, while normally sensitive to popular will in a generalized sense, not unduly so. While elected officials could not ignore the views of their constituents on local matters, the political system has nonetheless given considerable latitude to elected representatives to follow presidential or party leadership on most policy issues, and presidents have often taken the unpopular course where they believed it to be right.

This relative freedom to follow presidential or party leadership at the national level has been a function of political parties. Although American political parties have never enjoyed the ideological orientation, the discipline, or the responsibility of parties in a parliamentary system, they have traditionally been the link between citizens and government. And that link has been vital not merely in the election process, but more important, in the conduct of government itself. That fact is crucial. There is no question that the party structure is weakened today to the point that in national elections for the president—and to only a slightly lesser degree, statewide elections for governors and senators—we have today essentially a no-party system. Not only has television played a major role in destroying the role of the political party in such elections, but it has to a large degree become the substitute means linking citizens to government. And this fact has vast consequences.

Like our federal system itself, political parties have been highly decentralized entities operating almost exclusively at a state level. Their purpose has been to control public office by getting candidates identified with, and selected by, the party organization elected to public office at city, county, state, and congressional levels and, every four years, a president. They have served traditionally (and always with some exceptions) as an organization through which candidates for public office were channeled, which they served, and to which they owed the offices to which they aspired. Parties provided campaign funds, got out the vote, mobilized support for candidates, and nurtured party identification among citizens.

Our two-party political system is, of course, the creature of our electoral system—the state winner-take-all requirement coupled with the need for a majority of electoral votes to elect a president. This fact has created the need within the states to maintain the party label without, of course, any need to insist upon rigorous ideological commitment and conformity. The national party became a loose confederation of state and local party leaders who got together in convention every four years to negotiate the presidency and a platform. After nominating a candidate, they planned and executed, in collaboration with the candidate, campaign strategy and mobilized local party members to campaign, secure financial contributions, and turn out the vote on election day. Thereafter, so far as national politics was concerned, the parties went largely into hibernation for three years leaving matters to the president and party leaders in Congress.

Although this two-party system provided vigorous competition and choice, it did not require sharp ideological differences between the parties nor, for that matter, did it encourage or require an issue-oriented (on a national basis) or well-informed electorate. In terms of ideology there was little cohesion within a party and modest differences between the parties. It was a system that encouraged compromise and a centrist, often rather vague view in which quite profound ideological differences existed among members of the same party and were ignored, or obfuscated, by the unifying force of the common goal of gaining office. Importantly, there was little opportunity in this system, at a national level particularly, for one-issue politics—and efforts in this regard were normally dealt with and diffused by the party in its platform rather than by the candidates for office who were thus spared the burden of blame. Those who passionately espoused divisive issues had no place to turn to other than the two parties. The third-party alternative was quite impractical.

The issues of concern to candidates and to elected officials other than the president have historically been those of local or regional concern. Thus, candidates from the metropolitan Northeast shared relatively little with candidates from the farm-belt, the agricultural South, the oil states, and so forth. If the Democratic Party has been regarded as nationally more liberal and more welfare oriented in its ideology than the Republican Party, that was because its influence was greatest in metropolitan and industrialized areas; it courted union members and workers rather than businessmen or farmers, favored lower tariffs, and had a more blue-collar look and a somewhat greater ethnic mix from the melting-pot states. But the ideological span of both parties was enormous, for the Democrats were the single party of the Deep South and could ostensibly accommodate views as varied as those of FDR, Huey Long, Hubert Humphrey, and Theodore Bilbo. Essentially, the Republicans encompassed a similar span, and an observer from a European parliamentary system would have difficulty comprehending how such a party system could work at all, let alone quite well.

Although this political system may seem a far cry from the one created here in Philadelphia, it seems to me to have preserved many of its essential ingredients. The president had far more power, especially in times of crisis, than the Founding Fathers would have been comfortable with—but the separation of powers has checked any imperial presidency. The federal government also has far more power than the Framers intended, but given industrialization and American leadership in a smaller world, the political system has remained relatively decentralized. And, until recently, factions—a concern of the Founding Fathers—have not developed on ideological grounds because of the broad accommodation essential to a national party in a federal system. It has been a system in which everything could be compromised and ideology was an obstacle to success—thus, in some ways, a mirror image of the Convention itself. And, as V. O. Key noted, the party has been truly the web that bound the system together.

The most important aspect of this system was the connection between achieving office through party organization and governing through party organization. That connection made government not only possible but reasonably effective. Congress and the need to accommodate restrained presidents. Identification with political parties made it possible nonetheless for presidents to lead—albeit modestly—even absent a national crisis.

The decline of the political parties as the key to bridging the separation of congressional and presidential powers was taking place before the television explosion. But TV has greatly escalated this decline and left us as a nation with a series of problems that should concern us all.

Arguably, TV has made our political system far more democratic. The public is clearly more involved in candidate selection and issue orientation as political parties give way to the mass media as the linkage between voter and official. But it is far harder for our political system to adjust to this change than for the political parties in a parliamentary system, which is issue oriented. Our separation of powers, our fixed terms of office, and our decentralized governmental system all get in the way.

The three most serious problems posed by these changes are: First, the importance of money in the selection of candidates and the selection of issues—indeed, as "the primary arbiter of political outcomes," to borrow Senator Moynihan's phrase. The importance of money raises problems of buying votes on particular issues—something far too close to bribery in the guise of political contributions. The need of candidates for money to run campaigns—hugely expensive because of TV—gives access and influence to those who have it, whether directly through lobbying activities or indirectly by creating public opinion through the media. Obviously, money makes possible today single-issue—even fanatical—campaigns, which, as recent primaries demonstrate, can be successful. Almost certainly we will see an increase in lobbying connected with political contributions, in conflicts of interest, and in outright corruption.

Second, the problem of governing, of leadership. The political party provided a mechanism for nominating and electing candidates and it is that mechanism which television has weakened to the point of nonexistence. But the political party also provided a mechanism for governing. It may have been a fragile one on many issues and it certainly had none of the party discipline that goes with issue-oriented party politics. But the party label did create some interdependence among elected officials within the same organization and it did facilitate both presidential leadership and governmental decision. Defection for reasons of local or regional political concerns was understood and tolerated and the carrot was always more important than the stick in securing support. Further—and most important—the Senate and the House of Representatives had themselves sufficient party structure and organization and were sufficiently responsive to their own leadership to make the bargaining and negotiation necessary to workable coalitions possible. The absence of strongly held issue orientation as a political factor in holding office promoted consensus.

The third concern that I have is closely related to the first two. It arises out of the fact popular opinion can be manipulated and television is a powerful medium for doing so. Selling the presidency (or other office) like soap powder is distasteful but effective. It is much more likely to persuade than inform and it encourages both superficiality and a short attention span. Arguably, too, a generation brought up on the tube seeks easy solutions and instant gratification.

I am skeptical that TV can replace the party effectively as the web that makes our carefully constructed power-diffuse political system work. I do not think one can govern through television, and if I am wrong about that the problem is even more serious. A president would then have precisely the power to sway public emotion, which our Constitution—written in the Age of Reason—was designed to avoid.

We do not require Draconian measures to restore some workability in government by finding ways of strengthening our parties and weakening the bad influence of TV while preserving its important information function. The most difficult problem is probably that of controlling campaign finances because, to a large degree, the Supreme Court has equated money with free speech. But there are modest proposals afoot today that might do the job: increased government financing, allowing the political parties to become the principal conduits of public funds, a four-year term for Congressmen, and forbidding the thirty-second TV political commercial.

Time does not permit discussion in any detail of such proposals. My first point is that we must find ways of restoring the political parties in the capacity to bridge the separation of powers, albeit imperfectly. My second point is that we must harness the enormous potential of TV to inform and educate on political matters, not to sell candidates for office. It is my belief that the two go hand-in-hand, that both are doable, but that we had better not wait another century to do so.

* * *

*Speaker unknown.* The speaker did refer to the proposals for Constitutional reform. I wonder if he sees any place, for example, for such a change in having co-terminous elections in the House of Representatives.

*Nicholas Katzenbach.* I am fundamentally very conservative about changing the Constitution. And, indeed, if I look at the amendments we have made to the Constitution, I think with leaving out the first ten and the Civil War amendments, and leaving out the vote for women, we haven't done very much. So I am skeptical. I do think there is merit to some co-terminous elections. I think there may be some merit to a four-year term, but essentially I think we could restore things much closer to a working government, preserving all of the good features of the separation of powers, and they are good features, by getting a better handle on controlling funds and by making a conscious effort to strengthen the political parties. There are several proposals; for example, I would like to see the conventions left with some element of surprise to them. If we took all of the candidates for office in each party, and they had a free vote within the convention, we'd have 535 votes not accounted for in a primary election. There are a number of interesting provisions of that kind that don't require Constitutional amendments, and I would certainly like to exhaust those possibilities before drafting a Constitutional amendment that then might not work.

*Preston Cloud.* What is your opinion about the advantages and disadvantages of a single term for the president of six or eight years?

*Nicholas Katzenbach.* I don't think the single term of six years is good. I think we made a mistake in limiting the president to two four-year terms. If you have workable political parties, then I don't want to take anything away from the ability of the president to be a major factor in the governance of his own political party, and, of course, the two-term limitation tended to cut that out. It was a reaction, and a very understandable reaction, to FDR. I don't know what my colleagues speaking up here would think, but I would say despite my enormous admiration for him, he exercised far too much power—admittedly in times of crisis. I think it was just a reaction to that which led to the two-term limitation. I think it was unnecessary. I would get rid of it, except for the fact that amending the Constitution is so difficult.

*Herbert S. Bailey, Jr.* Given the first amendment, how would it be possible to ban the sixty-second commercials?

*Nicholas Katzenbach.* You can certainly ban them off network television. You've got a regulated industry there, and it seems to me you could either ban them or you could make them so difficult, you could say, "We'll do sixty-second commercials, but you've got to be live." "You've got to make it yourself." I would even experiment with saying, "You can have a sixty-second commercial, but you can't have a lot of other people talking on it; we want to see the candidate." I don't think sixty seconds is long enough. I think television can expose weaknesses but it can't expose weaknesses in a thirty- or sixty-second commercial that a candidate can spend two days making under close direction until he gets it right.

# *Reflections on the First Amendment: The Evolution of the American Jurisprudence of Free Expression*

**GEOFFREY R. STONE**

*Dean and Harry Kalven, Jr.*
*Professor of Law, University of Chicago*

The American jurisprudence of free expression is a rich tapestry of complex and occasionally inconsistent principles and doctrines that at any point in time are at different stages of evolution. Most of these doctrines have been forged in the heat of profound political and social controversies. I would like to note a few of these controversies and to point out the ways in which they have shaped some of the central principles upon which our First Amendment jurisprudence rests.

The first of these controversies involved the prosecution of individuals who agitated against the war and the draft during World War I. Although it is often forgotten today, many citizens were hostile to our entry into the European conflict. More than three hundred thousand men attempted to evade the draft and antiwar protests were common. To deal with such dissent, Congress enacted the Espionage Act of 1917, which made it unlawful for any person to obstruct the recruiting service of the United States, and the Sedition Act of 1918, which made it unlawful for any person to utter any disloyal language with the intent of opposing the cause of the United States.

During the war years, federal authorities prosecuted approximately two thousand individuals under these Acts. Typical of these individuals was Frank Shaffer, who was indicted in 1919 for mailing a publication that declared: "The war is wrong. Its prosecution will be a crime. There is not a question raised, an issue involved, a cause at stake, which is worth the life of one blue-jacket on the sea or one khaki-coat in the trenches."[1]

---

[1] *Shaffer v. United States*, 255 Fed. 886 (9th Cir. 1919).

In convicting defendants like Shaffer, the federal courts reasoned that the natural tendency of speech condemning the war was to "cause" refusals of induction, for an individual who is persuaded that the war is immoral is more likely to refuse induction than an individual who believes in the justness of the cause. Moreover, the courts rejected the claim that the intent of individuals like Shaffer was not to counsel law violation, but to achieve change through the lawful political process, by invoking the established legal principle that an individual may be held to intend the natural and foreseeable consequences of his acts. The courts also gave short shrift to the claim that such convictions violated the First Amendment, reasoning that a prohibition of speech that tends to cause unlawful conduct does not "abridge" the "freedom of speech" within the meaning of the First Amendment. Writing in 1920, Professor Zechariah Chafee observed that under this view of the law all genuine discussion among civilians of the justice and wisdom of continuing a war becomes perilous.[2]

In a series of decisions in 1919 and 1920, the Supreme Court of the United States embraced the twin doctrines of bad tendency and constructive intent and held that convictions for subversive advocacy did not violate the First Amendment.[3] In reaching these results, the Court explained that it "would be a travesty on the constitutional privilege" to assign defendants like Shaffer "its protection."[4]

As these decisions make clear, less than seventy years ago there was as a practical matter no genuinely effective, legally enforceable right to freedom of speech in the United States. In a series of eloquent dissenting opinions beginning in the fall of 1919, however, Justices Oliver Wendell Holmes and Louis Brandeis initiated a powerful counter-tradition within the Court. Listen to Justice Holmes, dissenting in *Abrams v. United States*,[5] in which the Court upheld the convictions of a group of Russian-Jewish emigrés who had thrown anti-war leaflets from the roof of a building in the lower East Side of New York:

> Persecution for the expression of opinion seems to me perfectly logical. . . . But when men have realized that time has upset many fighting faiths, they may come to believe even more than they believe the very foundations of their own conduct that the ultimate good desired is better

[2] See Z. Chafee, *Free Speech in the United States*, 36–108 (1941).
[3] See, e.g., *Schenck v. United States*, 249 U.S. 47 (1919); *Frohwerk v. United States*, 249 U.S. 204 (1919); *Debs v. United States*, 249 U.S. 211 (1919).
[4] *Gilbert v. Minnesota*, 254 U.S. 325 (1920).
[5] 250 U.S. 616 (1919).

> reached by free trade in ideas—that the best test of truth is the power of the thought to get itself accepted in the competition of the market, and that truth is the only ground upon which their wishes safely can be carried out. That at any rate is the theory of our Constitution. It is an experiment, as all life is an experiment. Every year if not every day we have to wager our salvation upon some prophecy based upon imperfect knowledge. While that experiment is part of our system I think that we should be eternally vigilant against attempts to check the expression of opinions that we loathe and believe to be fraught with death, unless they so imminently threaten immediate interference with the lawful and pressing purposes of the law that an immediate check is required to save the country.

The issue posed in the World War I cases implicates values at the very core of First Amendment concern. Although the Court in this era embraced a narrow view of the freedom of speech, it was the dissenting opinions of Justices Holmes and Brandeis that ultimately won the day. In the fifty years after Abrams, the Court, in a series of decisions involving the rights of syndicalists and anarchists in the 1920s and '30s and Communists in the 1950s and '60s, gradually moved toward the Holmes–Brandeis approach.[6] Finally, in its 1969 decision in *Brandenburg v. Ohio*,[7] the Court, echoing the Holmes–Brandeis dissents, declared in no uncertain terms that the First Amendment does not permit the Government to proscribe subversive advocacy unless such "advocacy is directed to inciting . . . imminent lawless action and is likely to incite . . . such action."

This evolution of First Amendment doctrine from 1919 to 1969 was premised on two fundamental principles. First, the government may *never* restrict the expression of particular ideas because it fears that citizens may adopt those ideas in the political process. As Professor Alexander Meikeljohn explained, this principle is rooted "in the very foundations of the self-governing process," for when "men govern themselves, it is they—and no one else—who must pass judgment upon unwisdom, unfairness and danger." Under this view, "no suggestion of policy" may be denied a hearing "because someone in control thinks it unwise, unfair, or un-American."[8]

Now, there is an anomaly in this principle that should not pass unnoticed. As Meiklejohn explained, this principle lies deep within the "foundations of the self-governing process." But if the essential goal is to preserve self-governance, why can't citizens, acting in their capacity as self-governors,

---

[6]See, e.g., *Gitlow v. New York*, 268 U.S. 652 (1925); *Whitney v. California*, 274 U.S.
[7]357 (1927); *Dennis v. United States*, 341 U.S. 494 (1951), 395 U.S. 444 (1969).
[8]See A. Meiklejohn, *Free Speech and Its Relation to Self-Government* (1948).

decide that certain policies are simply out of bounds and thus prohibit further debate on such issues? Under this view, it is not the government, as some independent entity, that is closing off debate, but citizens themselves, and they are doing so through the very self-governing process that the First Amendment is designed to promote.

The answer, I think, is that the First Amendment, which was itself adopted through the self-governing process, places out of bounds any law that attempts to freeze public debate at a particular moment in time. Under this view, a majority at any moment has the power to decide an issue of policy for itself, but it has no power irrevocably to decide that issue for future citizens by preventing them from continuing to debate the issue. This is, of course, what Justice Holmes described as the great First Amendment "experiment." It is, as Holmes recognized, a dangerous experiment. But it is, in the end, the central premise of the American constitutional system.

The second principle that emerges from the subversive advocacy cases is that the government may not restrict the expression of particular ideas merely because such expression might "cause" others to engage in unlawful conduct or otherwise threaten legitimate governmental interests. This principle is distinct from the first. The first principle holds that the government has no constitutionally legitimate interest in preventing citizens from hearing ideas because the government believes that such ideas might produce unwise decisions in the political process. The second principle holds that the Government may not suppress the expression of particular ideas even if that expression might in fact "cause" others to engage in acts that the government unquestionably has a right to prevent.

This second principle is premised upon two judgments. First, the second principle is an essential adjunct to the first. As Holmes observed, "persecution for the expression of opinion" is "perfectly logical." There is, in other words, a significant risk that the government's real objection to criticism of the war is not that such criticism might cause refusals of induction, but that it might turn citizens against the war in the political process. To suppress such unwise expression, and to circumvent the first principle, the government might simply assert that its objective in enacting and enforcing the Espionage and Sedition Acts is not to suppress subversive advocacy, but to prevent refusals of induction. If we are to preserve the first principle, we must guard against these sorts of pretextual evasions. The Holmes–Brandeis clear-and-present-danger standard provides an indirect but effective means of ferreting out such improper motivations, for it permits the government to restrict the expression of particular points of view only when it can demonstrate that such restrictions are essential to achieve compelling governmental interests.

The second principle rests on another rationale as well. Laws that restrict the expression of particular points of view are problematic, wholly apart from the motivation of the legislators, because, in Meiklejohn's words, they "mutilate the thought processes of the community." That is, even if the government is in fact attempting to prevent refusals of induction rather than to suppress criticism of the war, a law that bans such criticism severely distorts public debate by permitting the proponents of only one side of the debate to state their case. A law having this effect may be upheld only if the harm caused by the speech outweighs the harm caused by its suppression. Because a law that attempts to suppress a particular point of view does extraordinary harm to public debate and to the democratic process, such a law must be invalidated unless the government can demonstrate not only that the speech has a tendency to cause harm, but that the danger is clear, present, and grave. The critical point of the second principle, then, is that the First Amendment demands that we tolerate even potentially dangerous ideas unless the harm caused by the speech clearly outweighs the harm caused by its suppression.

The subversive advocacy cases thus yield two important principles. First, the government may not restrict the expression of particular ideas because it does not trust citizens to deal wisely with those ideas in the political process. And second, the government may not restrict the expression of particular ideas merely because such expression might cause others to engage in unlawful or otherwise undesirable acts. Rather, to restrict the expression of particular ideas, the government must demonstrate that the expression "so imminently threatens immediate interference with the lawful and pressing purposes of the law that an immediate check is required."

The issue posed in the subversive advocacy cases is central to our First Amendment jurisprudence. But it is not the only First Amendment issue and the principles that emerged from that controversy do not necessarily govern all First Amendment problems. To the contrary, the evolution of First Amendment doctrine reflects an ongoing effort of the Court to come to grips with shifting historical necessities. Over time, the Court has not only reconsidered its own earlier decisions, but has encountered new and different controversies that have called for the emergence of new and ever more refined First Amendment principles.

In the 1930s and '40s, it was the Jehovah's Witnesses, with their often vehement proselytizing, who generated the most important First Amendment issues. In these decisions, the Court recognized two important limitations on the principles that emerged from the subversive advocacy cases.

In *Chaplinsky v. New Hampshire*,[9] decided in 1942, Chaplinsky, a Jehovah's Witness, denounced all religion as a "racket." This led to a disturbance. As the city marshal escorted him from the scene, Chaplinsky called him a "God damned racketeer" and a "damned Fascist." For this language, Chaplinsky was prosecuted and convicted under a fighting-words statute, which prohibited any person to call any other person "by an offensive or derisive name." Chaplinsky maintained that this conviction violated the First Amendment.

The Supreme Court, in a unanimous decision, rejected Chaplinsky's claim. The Court explained that there "are certain well-defined and narrowly limited classes of speech," such as "the lewd and obscene, the profane, the libelous, and the insulting or 'fighting' words," which "are no essential part of any exposition of ideas and are of such slight social value as a step to truth" that their "prevention and punishment . . . have never been thought to raise any Constitutional problem."

The Court in *Chaplinsky* thus recognized that there are some classes of speech that are of such low First Amendment value that they can be regulated or even prohibited without satisfying the clear-and-present-danger standard. It is on the basis of this theory that the Court has upheld restrictions, not only of fighting words, but of libel, obscenity, commercial advertising, and child pornography.

It is important to note, however, that there has been an important evolution in this area of First Amendment jurisprudence, analogous to the evolution in the area of subversive advocacy. In its early decisions, the Court held that low value speech is entirely outside the protection of the First Amendment—it simply is not within "the freedom of speech" that is protected by the Constitution. In its more recent decisions, the Court has employed a form of categorical balancing, through which it defines the precise circumstances in which each category of low value speech may be restricted.

Although the determination that any particular type of expression is "of such slight social value as a step to truth" that it is not worthy of full First Amendment protection is not without difficulty, the low-value doctrine has, on balance, served a salutary function. It has operated as a useful safety valve, enabling the Court to deal sensibly with somewhat harmful but relatively unimportant speech without diluting the protection it accords speech at the very heart of the constitutional guarantee.

---

[9] 315 U.S. 568 (1942).

The second limitation recognized in the Jehovah's Witness cases is illustrated by the Court's 1941 decision in *Cox v. New Hampshire*[10] In Cox, several Jehovah's Witnesses were convicted of violating a state law prohibiting any procession upon a public street without first obtaining a permit. Although such a law clearly could not pass muster under the Holmes–Brandeis clear-and-present-danger standard, the Court nonetheless upheld the statute, noting that the permit requirement was designed to enable public authorities to regulate the time, place, and manner of expression.

The critical fact that distinguished *Cox* from the subversive advocacy cases is that the law in *Cox* restricted expression without regard to the message conveyed. Such content-neutral restrictions are commonplace. Consider, for example, laws that restrict noisy speeches near a hospital, or ban billboards in residential communities, or limit campaign contributions, or prohibit the mutilation of draft cards. Because such laws are neutral with respect to content, they are not as likely to distort public debate or to be tainted by improper motivation as laws that expressly restrict only particular points of view. Thus, as the Court implicitly recognized in *Cox*, content-neutral laws need not be tested by the clear-and-present-danger standard.

The content-based/content-neutral distinction plays a central role in modern First Amendment theory, for in dealing with content-neutral restrictions, the Court invokes not the clear-and-present-danger standard, but a form of ad hoc balancing, through which it varies the standard of review according to the extent to which each particular restriction actually limits the opportunities for free expression. Like the low-value doctrine, the content-neutral doctrine has served a useful function, for it enables the Court to maintain a highly skeptical approach to those laws that most seriously threaten core First Amendment values, while at the same time according greater deference to legislative judgment when dealing with laws that less directly threaten those values.

The next controversy to confront the Court arose during the anti-Communist era of the 1950s and '60s. In these cases, the Court considered a wide range of laws designed to restrict the activities of the Communist Party. Some of these cases involved direct criminal prosecutions of members of the Party and thus raised questions similar to those posed in the World War I cases.

But the cases of this era also involved two quite different types of restrictions which posed a new challenge to the ingenuity of First Amendment doctrine. First, in some of these cases, the government denied public employment to individuals because of their past or present membership in the Commu-

[10] 312 U.S. 569 (1941).

nist Party. The government maintained that such restrictions should be tested by a more deferential standard than laws that criminally punish Communist activity because government employment is not a right, but a privilege. Thus, the government argued that even if it could not directly prohibit subversive advocacy, it was surely free not to employ individuals who belonged to subversive organizations.

Second, in other cases, the government engaged in legislative investigations of the Communist Party to determine whether legislation might be necessary to protect the national security. The Government maintained that such investigations posed only a tangential First Amendment issue, for the investigations themselves did not directly punish individuals for their speech or association.

In its earliest decisions addressing these issues, the Supreme Court sided with the government. Over time, however, the Court came to embrace a more speech-protective approach. In the employment cases, the Court came to understand that for government to use the lever of public employment as a means to reward or penalize political activity could have drastic consequences for public debate, especially in an era of ever-expanding government. The Court therefore held that an individual could be denied public employment because of his associations only if the government could prove that the individual had joined an organization that had unlawful aims and that, in joining that organization, the individual had the "specific intent" to advance those aims.[11]

Similarly, in the legislative investigation cases, the Court came to understand that the public exposure of unpopular political activities can chill the freedom of speech and association in much the same way as criminal punishment. It therefore held that the government has no right to expose for the sake of exposure and that the government cannot require the disclosure of Communist Party membership without first showing a "substantial relation between the information sought and a subject of overriding and compelling state interest."[12]

In the 1960s, the Court confronted another set of issues, which arose out of the civil rights demonstrations of that era. In *Edwards v. South Carolina*,[13] 180 black students marched to the South Carolina State House to protest discrimination. A crowd of about 300 whites observed the demonstration. After about thirty minutes, local law enforcement authorities ordered the

---

[11] See, e.g., *Elfbrandt v. Russell*, 384 U.S. 11 (1966).
[12] *Gibson v. Florida Legislative Investigating Committee*, 372 U.S. 539 (1963).
[13] 372 U.S. 229 (1963).

demonstrators to disperse. When they refused to do so, they were arrested for breach of the peace. The state maintained that the dispersal was necessary to preserve the public peace and to prevent a possible riot. The state argued further that this case was a far cry from the subversive advocacy cases, for unlike the Espionage Act of 1917 and the Sedition Act of 1918, the South Carolina breach-of-the-peace law was not directed against any particular point of view.

The Supreme Court overturned the convictions. In reaching this result, the Court declared that the Constitution does not permit a state to make criminal the peaceful expression of unpopular views and that the government may not restrict speech merely because it stirs people to anger, invites dispute, or brings about a condition of unrest. Rather, in such circumstances, the government must take all reasonable steps to protect the speech. If anyone is to be dispersed, it is the threatening and unruly onlookers, not the speakers.

In these decisions, the Court recognized the dangers of what Professor Harry Kalven called the "heckler's veto." Just as the Court came to understand in the subversive advocacy cases that the government may not legitimately restrict expression because of a paternalistic judgment that its citizens should not be permitted to hear what it regards as unwise or dangerous ideas, so, too, did it understand in the civil rights cases of the 1960s that the government may not legitimately restrict expression because of the intolerant judgment of some citizens that other citizens should not be permitted to express ideas that they regard as dangerous or unwise. The government, in other words, can no more permit one group of citizens to censor another than censor them itself.

The American jurisprudence of free expression is a patchwork of doctrines and principles. These doctrines have emerged over time. They are the product of a lively, dynamic, and evolving debate within the Court both within and across generations. The central metaphor of our First Amendment jurisprudence remains Justice Holmes's "marketplace of ideas." There is no more vital marketplace of ideas than the Supreme Court itself.

* * *

*John Wheeler.* The place of television in the Vietnam War is well known. If television had existed at the time of the American Civil War, and the northern public had seen the bloodiness of the battles and had thus reacted against the war, would Lincoln have been justified in turning off television?

*Geoffrey Stone*. No!

*Speaker unknown*. In the period after WWII there was an attempt to outlaw organizers of the Communist Party on the ground that it was a felony to conspire to advocate the violent overthrow of government. Is that another classic case?

*Geoffrey Stone*. You're referring to prosecutions under the Smith Act. These prosecutions posed a special difficulty in understanding the concept of "clear and present danger," for those prosecutions were typically for conspiracy to advocate. Now, it's a nonsequitur to talk about a "clear and present danger" of overthrow of the government if the charge is conspiring to advocate the overthrow of government. That was one of the things the Court wrestled with in the Dennis case in 1951, without much success. In the Dennis case, which involved the prosecution of the leaders of the Communist Party under the Smith Act, the Court for the first time expressly embraced the Holmes–Brandeis concept of "clear and present danger" in the subversive advocacy context, but then proceeded to interpret "clear and present danger" as meaning that as the gravity of the evil goes up—and violent revolution is obviously a very grave danger—the clarity and presence of the danger necessary to restrict speech can go down. As Harry Kalven put it, the Court, from the standpoint of Holmes and Brandeis, snatched defeat from the jaws of victory.

*Erwin Griswold*. Can I supplement the question about television in wartime? Suppose that the president as Commander-in-Chief directed his generals to kick television off the battlefield. How would you answer that one?

*Geoffrey Stone*. The question concerns access to information rather than the ability to communicate information once one obtains it. It is an extremely difficult line to draw. If, as is often said by the press, the public has a "right to know," the logical conclusion is not only that the press has a right to publish, but that it has a right to obtain information so that the public can know. But that may prove too much. What it suggests, for example, is that the Freedom of Information Act is constitutionally mandated. The compromise that the Court has adopted has been described by Alexander Bickel as an uneasy one in which the press is allowed to publish just about anything it can get its hands on, but the government is allowed to do just about whatever it wants to keep the press from getting the information. Under this view, which doesn't work badly in practice, this kind of crude accommodation will result in a reasonable compromise of the competing interests without having a court try to figure out what type of access to information is constitutionally mandated. Basically, the point is that the government is not very good at keeping secrets and in keeping information away from the press. It will succeed in doing so, at least for any appreciable period of time, only if the government's interest in keeping the matter secret is extraordinarily grave, in which case it probably should be allowed to keep it secret.

*Milton Friedman.* You've given a very interesting presentation of the decisions. You indicated, though, an emphasis on the benefits that would be obtained by permitting particular types of speech. Now, I think one would also want to consider the amount of cost involved in permitting that speech. Take commercial speech. The benefits may be small but presumably the costs may be generally small, too. On the other hand, if you look at speech criticizing the draft during a war, it obviously raises an important and legitimate question about whether the war should be fought. But the cost can be immense if we are paralyzed from conducting an activity for the survival of the country. How do you balance those two? If we look at only the benefits, large or small, they aren't really sufficient to making a relevant decision about whether speech should be permitted.

*Geoffrey Stone.* That is exactly right. What we have is a judgment, benefits versus costs. The interesting question about commercial advertising is how to define the benefits, not from the standpoint of society, but from the standpoint of the purposes of the First Amendment. There are those who believe that speech is speech, and whether it's commercial speech, political speech, or entertainment makes no difference at all to the First Amendment. Under this view, the value of all speech to the purposes of the First Amendment is identical, and therefore commercial advertising should be accorded the same protection, should be regarded as providing the same benefit, as political speech. Others, following *Chaplinsky*, reason that there are some types of expression that are within the definitional concept of "speech" but are not within the First Amendment concept of "speech," because they are not related to political matters. Under this view, because commercial advertising is only very tangentially related to politics, it's entitled to only protection. Its benefits from a first Amendment perspective are relatively slight, and a much lower level of cost would therefore be sufficient to justify its restriction.

# *The United States Constitution as Social Compact*

LOUIS HENKIN

Thanks largely, I think, to John Rawls's "A Theory of Justice," the social contract has assumed a prominent place in contemporary political theory. As we celebrate the bicentennial of the United States Constitution, it is interesting to consider the Constitution as social compact. I do so under the following headings: Was the Constitution a valid social compact? Is the Constitution a social compact today? What were—what are—the terms of that compact? What are the implications, if any, of considering the Constitution a social compact?

## 1.

The Constitution does not explicitly espouse any political theory. In that respect, it differs from the other political instruments that comprise our national hagiography. The Declaration of Independence; the Virginia Bill of Rights on which the Declaration drew; the other state bills, declarations, and constitutions that were inspired by Jefferson's Declaration, all were explicitly committed to a theory of government—to the social compact.

The Declaration of Independence justified the exercise by the colonists of "self-determination" by invoking a theory of government, one so deeply and widely held as to be a truth that was self-evident. In these precincts it is doubtless supererogatory to quote what every schoolchild has learned by heart:

> We hold these truths to be self-evident, that all men are created equal, that they are endowed by their Creator with certain unalienable Rights, that among these are Life, Liberty and the pursuit of Happiness. That to secure these rights, Governments are instituted among Men, deriving their just powers from the consent of the governed,—That whenever any Form of Government becomes destructive of these ends, it is the Right

> of the People to alter or to abolish it, and to institute new Government, laying its foundation on such principles and organizing its powers in such form, as to them shall seem most likely to effect their Safety and Happiness.

Legitimate government results when individuals band together to establish a government to secure their natural rights. The legitimacy of the government rests on the consent of the governed. The people may alter or abolish their government at will.

Jefferson was articulating the political principles that were in the *Zeitgeist* of the eighteenth century on the American continent. Those principles are the essence of American constitutionalism. They are not expressed in the United States Constitution, but only, I believe, because of the particular genealogy of that instrument.

The United States Constitution, we know, emerged from a process designed to amend the Articles of Confederation. The Articles were a treaty establishing a federation of states; they were not a constitution for a government, and therefore did not articulate or reflect any theory of government. Instead of amending the Articles, the Convention framed a constitution for a "government of the United States." But the new government was designed to be "a more perfect union," not a full-fledged government in the spirit of the Declaration, designed and instituted "to secure these rights." The task of securing the rights of individuals was to remain the responsibility of the governments of the individual states. For their purposes—to form a more perfect union—the Framers saw no need to articulate any theory of government, as they saw no need to include a bill of rights. Later, the lack of a bill of rights proved to be a cause of wide concern, and the addition of a bill of rights became a condition of ratification. The lack of an explicit theory of government was not a cause of concern; none has been added.

Alone among the early American constitutions, then, the Constitution of the United States remains without explicit commitment to the American theory of government—to natural rights anteceding government, popular sovereignty as the source of political authority, government by social compact, the consent of the governed as the justification of government. But although not fully articulated, the commitment to social contract is reflected in the instrument concluded in Philadelphia in 1787. When it was decided that a more perfect union required not a confederation of states but a new government, the articles of agreement among the states, prepared and signed by "the undersigned Delegates of the States," were replaced by a constitution ordained and established by the only legitimate source of authority for a government, "We the people."

The commitment of the Framers and of their generation to the principles of the Declaration is implied also in the amendments we now call the Bill of Rights, adopted and ratified within two years of the birth of the new Constitution. The Bill of Rights does not grant rights; it protects pre-existing, natural rights. Congress shall make no law abridging "*the* freedom of speech." "*The right* of the people to be secure in their persons, houses, papers, and effects . . . shall not be violated." The Ninth and Tenth Amendments are explicit: "The enumeration in the Constitution of certain rights shall not be construed to deny or disparage others *retained* by the people." "The powers not delegated to the United States . . . are *reserved* to the States respectively, or to the people." (Emphasis added.)

The United States Constitution, I believe, was—became—an authentic expression of the principles of American constitutionalism articulated in the Declaration of Independence and the state constitutions of the time—a social contract.

## 2

"We the people" of 1787–89 ordained and established the Constitution. The authenticity of that assertion has not passed unquestioned. The delegates to what later was called the "Constitutional Convention" were chosen by state legislatures whose members were elected by the votes of only a small percentage of the population. The constitution which the delegates produced—exceeding their delegated authority to amend the Articles of Confederation—was ratified by representatives of only a small percentage of the population, and by narrow (in some instances questionable) majorities.

Clearly, our political ancestors were Republicans, not Democrats. For them, "the people" did not mean all the inhabitants of the land, or even all of its citizens; the people consisted of those white males qualified for self-government by intelligence, "virtue," commitment (as manifested by ownership of sufficient property). The majority of the population—women, slaves, free blacks, persons without substantial property—had no voice in ordaining the Constitution. Were they not part of "the people"? Were they deemed to be represented by the few who had the right to vote, as married women were said to be represented by their husbands?

There are even more serious difficulties in justifying the government of 1789 et seq. under Jefferson's second principle: The just powers of government are derived from the consent of the governed. If the un-enfranchised majority of the population were not part of "the people" entitled to participate in instituting government, surely they were among the governed. Since they had no vote, in what sense did they consent? Except for slaves (and in a different sense married women), they were free to leave—if they had a place to go and the means to leave, if the various costs of leaving were not so exorbitant as to render their freedom to leave questionable. (After the Revolution, many had in fact left for England or Canada.) Did those who stayed "decide to stay"? Did they appreciate that by staying they were consenting? Did they understand what they were consenting to?

## 3.

Questions about "the people" who originally ordained the Constitution, and about the consent of the governed in 1789, pale beside challenges to the continuing legitimacy of the Constitution and to the authenticity of the consent of the governed thereafter. Jeffersonian social contract theory, it would seem, requires that government be instituted or reconfirmed and maintained by the people in each generation. (For that reason, perhaps, Jefferson wrote that a constitution has a life of nineteen years.) Jeffersonian theory requires the consent of the people who are being governed at any time, not merely the consent of their ancestors.

The constitutional system ordained by the people of 1787–89 has been imposed on those born or arriving here since 1789. For them, there has been no opportunity to ordain and establish a constitution for their governance; for them, constitutional change has been possible only in accordance with pre-prescribed, difficult procedures for constitutional amendment. Under the theory to which the Framers were committed, if the Constitution of 1789 is the Constitution of later generations—our Constitution—it must be because later generations adopt the Constitution, at least by acquiescence. Perhaps, those who came to the United States voluntarily, knowingly, can be said to have accepted the Constitution and the constitutional system which they found; for those born here, acceptance would have to be deemed to be implied in their continued residence here after they came of age.

Again, the authenticity of that consent is suspect. Most of them—many of us—do not fully appreciate what we have consented to. We do not know what is in the Constitution, surely not all that the courts have found there. Many of us do not appreciate our right and ability to leave. Many cannot in fact leave, and during some periods of war or emergency departure is forbidden by law. In any event, is consent present and authentic when there is only choice between departure and submission? Are we to be deemed to consent as long as we do not join to exercise "the right of the people to alter or to abolish it," our Jeffersonian right of revolution?

The continuing consent of the governed has become less questionable. Finally we have become a democracy. Slowly, in the past 100 years, exclusions from suffrage were eliminated: Exclusion on account of race was forbidden by the Fifteenth Amendment (1870); on account of gender, by the Nineteenth (1919); on account of failure to pay a tax, by the Twenty-fourth (1962); on account of age (for persons over 18), by the Twenty-sixth Amendment (1971). More important, by creative construction (some might say distortion) of the Fourteenth Amendment only some twenty years ago, we have moved from eliminating grounds for exclusion to affirming a right to equal universal suffrage in principle for all citizens. "The people" today are all the people, at least all citizens. Consent of the governed has finally come to mean all the governed, at least all citizens. Today only the noncitizen is governed without an opportunity to participate in government, and in general he can acquire that equal opportunity readily by becoming a citizen.

## 4.

If the Constitution was—is—a social compact, who are the parties to the compact, and what are its terms?

The Declaration of Independence and the state constitutions contemplated two different compacts: by the first compact, the people agree among themselves to form a government; a second compact, between the people and the government they create, binds the agencies of government to respect the blueprint of government and the rights retained by the people.

As regards the United States Constitution, the compact among the people to create a government of the United States is implied in the preambular phrase: "We the people . . . do ordain and establish this Constitution." There is no other reference to that compact in the text of the Constitution.

It might be suggested that a compact to form a government implies other commitments among the people—a promise to each other to respect the government to be created, to abide by the laws (and to pay the taxes) enacted by the agreed government in accordance with agreed procedures. Also implicit in that compact, perhaps, is a commitment by the people to respect each other's antecedent rights. If such commitments are implied in the compact to form a government, there is no hint of them in the United States Constitution, and they are not part of our constitutional jurisprudence. A citizen cannot make a *constitutional* claim that another citizen is not fulfilling his or her obligations to pay taxes, or to observe the law, or to respect the rights of others. Although—Jefferson said—governments are instituted to secure life and liberty and other rights, the Constitution does not protect such rights against invasion by one's neighbor.

That principle has become part of our constitutional jurisprudence. It is only governmental action—"state action"—that the Constitution addresses and circumscribes. The failures of the people, and the failures of some of the people in respect for others, are not the concern of the Constitution. For a notable example, individual violations of the life, liberty, or property of other individuals, or private discriminations on grounds of race, religion, or gender, are not constitutional violations. It has required legislation to establish remedies against private invasions of rights, and for long the Constitution was construed as denying Congress the power to enact such civil rights legislation.

The United States Constitution, then, contains only the second compact, the compact between the people and their government. Our constitutional jurisprudence includes, and the courts will enforce, the blueprint of government ordained by the people: the reciprocal limitations between the states and the federal government, which we have come to call federalism; the respective spheres of the three branches of the federal government; the limitations on the authority of the federal branches and on the authority of the states that are set forth in the Constitution and the Amendments, notably in the Bill of Rights and the Fourteenth Amendment.

Strange to say, the compact between the government and the people does not include a commitment by government to carry out the purpose of government according to Jefferson—to secure our natural rights against our neighbors. An affirmative obligation to enact and execute civil rights acts and other laws to that end is not in the Constitution. Surely such an obligation is ordinarily not enforceable by the courts, which say what the Constitution means.

## 5.

The social compact between the people and their government is enforced by the courts, perhaps as surrogates for the people. But there is little talk of social contract in the jurisprudence, which the courts have derived from the Constitution. The courts have built their authority to enforce the Constitution in substantial part on the fact of a written Constitution; perhaps for that reason, they have felt obliged to stick close to the text, and there is not enough social contract in the text to make it serve jurisprudential purposes. Early, Justice Chase in 1798 (*Calder v. Bull*) and John Marshall in 1810 (*Fletcher v. Peck*) suggested that governments were bound to respect natural rights even if such rights are not expressed in the Constitution, but their colleagues insisted that, though governments were—naturally—obliged to respect natural rights, the courts had not been given authority to compel governments in the United States to do so. In our century, Justice Black warned against leaving courts at large with power to invoke natural rights to frustrate the policies of representative government. Distrust of the judiciary may largely explain the nullification of the Ninth Amendment as a textual basis for securing natural rights not enumerated in the Constitution.

Yet natural, inherent rights creep in, notably when the courts read the clause forbidding government to deprive a person of life, liberty, or property without due process of law as imposing substantive limitations. In particular, liberty was held to mean not only freedom from incarceration and the political–religious freedoms articulated in the First Amendment, but substantial autonomy and freedom from legislative regulation. Later, liberty was held to include a zone of autonomy in intimate matters, such as the right of persons to use contraceptives and the right of a woman to have an abortion. (It is not easy to understand the basis on which the Court refused to recognize that the right of privacy includes homosexual activities between consenting adults.)

## 6.

The United States Constitution has never been formally replaced or reordained, and it has hardly been amended. (The first ten amendments, the Bill of Rights, were the price of ratification, and in a real sense form part of the original package; except for the 13th, 14th, and 15th Amendments—the peace treaty of the Civil War, which abolished slavery, reshaped our Federalism, and extended protection for individual rights—constitutional amendments have not been fundamental.) If the Constitution is a social contract, if it is our social contract today, it is because "we the people" reordain our Constitution, informally, continually. If so, are the terms of our social contract only what they were in 1787 and during Reconstruction, only what is in the original text and its formal amendments? It has been suggested that the effect of constitutional ordainment should be accorded also to "constitutional outbursts," to expressions of the will of the people that are of constitutional dimension and import, such as the overwhelming vote for President Franklin Roosevelt and his Congress in 1936, effectively rejecting the rigid constitutional construction by which the Supreme Court had frustrated the early New Deal program. Might the people also ordain constitutional change tacitly, subtly—though it may not be easy to determine that the people had done so, except in retrospect?

There is strong evidence that in some respects the contemporary social contract has moved beyond constitutional text. Principally, the social compact represented by the constitutional text reflects eighteenth-century views of the purposes of government. Per Jefferson, the government of 1789 was instituted "to secure these rights," the rights which men and women had before government and apart from government—the natural inalienable rights, including notably life, liberty, and the pursuit of happiness. Two hundred years later the people look to government for larger purposes. Is it not the case that the people today have recognized and ordained that it is among the purposes of government to ensure to every inhabitant—as of right, not by grace and char-ity—basic human needs (food, shelter, health care, education) when the individual cannot provide them?

There has also been, I think, a change of constitutional character both in our conception of rights, in the catalogue of rights protected, and in the scope of particular rights. The Framers of the Fourteenth Amendment had limited views as to what they meant by the equal protection of the laws. For them, apparently, it did not mean that there could be no racial segregation in the schools. For them, perhaps, it did not mean that women could practice law equally with men. Our social contract, however, has rejected the view that a white majority can impose "separate but equal" schools. Our social contract recognizes the right of women to equal treatment, even if the country did not complete the formal procedures pursuant to Article V for an equal rights amendment.

Or, consider the clause prohibiting an establishment of religion. The Framers of the First Amendment—if we could agree on who they were—sought to prohibit an official church, and probably to prevent official preference for one Christian denomination over another. Jefferson and Madison talked of a wall of separation between Church and State, but it is not clear that they spoke for "the people" of their time; and what "the wall" meant for them is not obvious. Later, the people who ordained the Fourteenth Amendment may or may not have intended to make the Establishment Clause applicable to the states. But in 1940 the courts held that the Establishment Clause does apply to the states. In 1948, the Supreme Court converted the Jefferson–Madison metaphor of a wall of separation between church and state into constitutional principle. It may or may not be what the First and Fourteenth Amendments meant when they were ordained. It may or may not be what the Framers of these Amendments intended. But has it not been incorporated into the social contract of we the people—of an urban, religiously pluralist people, in the second half of the twentieth century?

## 7.

It may be that somewhere along the centuries we have dropped the ancestral commitment to social contract, that we maintain only a commitment to a fixed, inherited constitution. Or, perhaps we satisfy the original theory of our constitutionalism in that we the people today agree to ordain and establish the Constitution of 1787 (as formally amended) as our social contract. If we had a clearer idea as to the theory that justifies our living under a 200-year-old Constitution, we might have better guidance as we seek our way among the issues that agitate the constitutional universe.

I think we should take Jefferson seriously. Constitutionalism is better justified, I think, by contemporary social contract than by ancestor worship. If we remain committed to social contract, it is *our* social contract that matters more than that of our ancestors. We have maintained *their* text but we give it *our* meaning. We accept Article V, the Amendment clause, but we assert also the right to reinterpret the text interstitially without formal amendment. That, perhaps, is why there have been few formal amendments of moment.

Perhaps, in yet a third, ancillary, compact, we the people have accepted the Supreme Court as our surrogate for calibrating and updating the Constitution to reflect better the contemporary social compact. We have given that task to judges and, to protect ourselves against abuse by even that least dangerous branch, we continue to root the authority of the Justices in holy writ and frame the judicial mandate in constitutional text. We cabin our judges by the rules and traditions of judicial process; we insist that they act as judges, and that they work in the spirit and within the limits of the art of interpretation. But it is our compact they are determining. If we the people effectively reordain the Constitution in our generation, are we committed to the text as our ancestors wrote it, or as we read it? Are we committed to what the Framers intended by what they wrote, or to what we would make of it? Marshall stressed to his colleagues and their successors that it is a Constitution they were expounding. Should they not be reminded that it is *our* Constitution they are expounding?

In any event, our principal social compact is not with the judiciary, but with all of our government. "We the people" ought to be aware of, and insist on, our contemporary constitutional values. We ought to assure that government is instituted and maintained "to secure these rights" as we understand them, the rights identified by Jefferson, but also the rights we recognize and exalt today.

# *Reflections on the Supreme Court Appointment Process*

**HENRY J. ABRAHAM**

*James Hart Professor of Government and Foreign Affairs, University of Virginia*

## I.

We are prone to be critical of what Alexander Hamilton called "the least dangerous branch of the government"—a description that is best a half-truth—and we are entitled to be critical. Yet everything in this world is relative, and if our judiciary, with the Supreme Court at its apex, is not perfect (as a matter of fact, it is far from it!), well, as Charlie Brown suggests appropriately, nothing is! Still, the Court would appear to do rather well in the public's esteem or perception (whichever of the two may be the most apposite noun), with the most recent poll bearing witness to that happy fact: In that evaluative exercise, the usual "scientific"—I do hope it is/was—cross-section was asked, as it is annually, to render judgment on the merit or value or quality of visible professional groups in and out of government. As has been the case on almost all, although not all, occasions, the Court ranked higher than either of the other two branches in the eyes of the respondents. Parenthetically, let me report, not without glee, that the three bottom categories were: the lowest, labor unions; the next lowest, the legal profession (what delicious irony!); and the third lowest, Congress.

Be that as it may—I confess I love it—it is crystal clear that the public has considerable faith in our judicial branch, and by and large, in its personnel. With remarkable constancy, it views the bench, in particular the Supreme Court, with a degree of confidence that justifies Mr. Madison's sanguine plea for "a bench happily filled." On the whole, I believe the Court merits that appellation cum evaluation—notwithstanding some appointments that have deservedly given rise to blushing. Yet the vast majority of the 103 Justices who to date have served on our highest tribunal have consistently been accorded high ratings by Court-watchers and students, who have evinced a remarkable degree of agreement on individual performance.

John Jay.

Engraving by William S. Leney. Courtesy of the Library Company of Philadelphia.

Thus, the Blaustein–Mersky study of 1979 asked 65 law school deans, professors of law, history, and political science (including myself) to rank the 96 Justices who had served on the Court from 1789–1969 (just prior to Chief Justice Burger's appointment). Requested to confine ourselves to the demonstrably unfortunately open-ended categorizations of "great" (12), "near great" (15), "average" (55), "below average" (6), and "failures" (8), we collectively conferred the adjective "great" on twelve. (I selected only nine.) Chronologically, the twelve were John Marshall, Story, Taney, Harlan I, Holmes, Hughes, Brandeis, Stone, Cardozo, Black, Frankfurter, and Warren. Only one received all 65 votes: Marshall; #2 was Brandeis, with 62 votes; #3 Holmes, with 61; #4 Black, with 44; and #5 Frankfurter, with 41 votes. What is noteworthy is that these same twelve have appeared on each of the other four authentic published contemporary lists of rankings as "great," including Jerome Frank's, Felix Frankfurter's (he uncharacteristically modestly excluded himself); and two formal newspapers surveys.

In this age of statistics, word processors, computers, and Betamaxes, a few bits of data may be in order to characterize those who obtained the Nirvana of the highest tribunal of the land. The good news I have for those among this distinguished audience who happen to be attorneys, is that they are all theoretically eligible to be sent to the Court (unlike me, a mere critic of lawyers . . . although I want to report to you that my summer of 1981 was "made" by Arthur Selwyn Miller's gratuitous nomination of three political scientists to the Stewart vacancy: my colleagues Walter F. Murphy of Princeton University and John R. Schmidhauser of the University of Southern California [he was once a Democratic member of Congress from Iowa's First District] and myself). The Divine Afflatus was upon me; but we are all still waiting to hear from 1600 Pennsylvania Avenue . . . despite Professor Miller's renewed nomination of us during the spring (though he dropped Professor Schmidhauser in favor of Professor Dean Alfange of the University of Massachusetts). (I asked our Law School Dean, Richard Merrill, whether he would trade in my two honorary LL.D.'s for one J.D., or even one LL.B., but he demurred.) Now the bad news that I have for those of you who may be potentially qualified—and you will admit that it constitutes a memorable piece of research—the *bad* news is that of all identifiable professional occupational groups, only symphony conductors have greater life expectancy than United States Supreme Court Justices!

Now, shall we take a look at those to sit on the Court to date (spring 1987)? The 102 men and the one woman were nominated by 35 presidents, with three—W. H. Harrison, Taylor, and Carter—having no opportunity to choose anyone at all, and one, Andrew Johnson, seeing his several efforts frustrated successfully by a hostile Senate. Not counting a mere refusal to act on nominations—of which there were several—that constitutional partner in the appointment process has so far formally rejected 27 presidential nominations to the Supreme Court, all but four of these (namely, lower federal court judges Parker, Haynsworth, and Carswell, and the aborted promotion of Justice Fortas to Chief Justice) coming in the nineteenth century. It ought to be noted, of course, that neither in law nor under the federal Constitution is a law degree required for membership on *any* level of the *federal* judiciary. Interestingly, only 56 of the 103 individuals who have served on the Court attended a law school and of those, only 39 were graduated therefrom. Indeed, it was not until 1845 that a sitting Supreme Court Justice had *attended* law school (Levi Woodbury, and for just one year). The first law school *graduate* to mount the Court was Benjamin Curtis in 1851. It was not until 1957—just a bit more than three decades ago—that the Supreme Court, for the first time, was composed *entirely* of law school graduates. The last Justice to serve *without* a law degree was Stanley F. Reed (Robert H. Jackson was next-to-last), and the last never to have attended law school at all was James F. Byrnes, who served from 1941 to 1942. Those 103 successful lawyer-appointees have come from ten major professional subgroups, led by 23 from the lower federal judiciary, and 22 each from the state judiciary and from diverse posts in the federal executive/administrative branch. Upon ascending to the high bench they *resided* in 31 different states, headed by 15 from New York, nine from both Ohio and Virginia, and eight from Massachusetts; 10 states have sent one; 19 none at all. The latter fact of political life prompted Republican Senator William ("Wild Bill") Langer of North Dakota, then a senior member of the Senate's Committee on the Judiciary, to commence in 1953 a campaign of opposition to any and all presidential nominees to the Court until his home state would receive a Supreme Court appointment. He went to his grave in 1959, his wish still unrealized—as it is to this day (spring 1987).

The acknowledged religious preferences of the 103 individual jurists fall into 12 different groups, the only ones in "double-digit-figures" being 27 Episcopalians, 25 avowedly unspecified Protestants, and 17 Presbyterians; there have been seven Roman Catholics, five Jews, and the balance have been specified other Protestant adherents. Five professed political party designations characterize the successful nominees, including one Whig, one Independent, 12 Federalists, 41 Republicans, and 48 Democrats. It would hence be wrong to stipulate an overwhelming partisan flavor for the high bench.

Such a flavor unmistakably, however, has informed the selection of nominees in terms of their political affiliation in concord with that of the nominating president. The lowest partisan percentage to date—and now necessarily counting *all* federal judges—has been earned by President Ford (81.2 percent Republican), the highest by President Washington (100 percent Federalist). The lowest partisan-correlation nomination percentage in *this* century for *all* federal judges is still President Ford's aforementioned 81.2 (President Taft's 82.2 being a close second), the highest that by the sole Ph.D. in political science so far to occupy the White House, Woodrow Wilson, who amassed a near perfect 98.6 percent score of Democratic appointees. More or less tied for the second highest correlative slot are Presidents Carter and Harding, with 97.8 Democratic and 97.7 Republican identifications, respectively; President Reagan was close behind as of his seventh year in office.

## II.

Indubitably, the profile and statistics just cited point to a broad-gauged commitment to a "representative" philosophy for judicial appointments with one third of President Carter's close to 300 appointees comprising women and minorities. An examination of the intention of the Founding Fathers on that always so lively controversial issue demonstrates with crystal clarity, however, that "representativeness" was not even considered, let alone advocated. Merit was the sole criterion on the mind of the delegates, in Philadelphia, "representativeness" being reserved to the legislature. The Founding Fathers of 1787 assumed as a matter of course that those appointed to the bench would be qualified. Merit was regarded as essential; "representativeness" did not even surface as an academic question—neither by the Federalists nor the Anti-Federalists, neither by the Madisonians nor by the Hamiltonians.

Yet if it was not an issue then, the concept of "representativeness" has assuredly become one, and increasingly so, in modern mold. Indeed, it is now a patently demonstrable fact of the life of government and politics that so-called "equitable considerations" in the selection and nominations to the bench have become not only omnipresent, but arguably omnipotent, in the decisional processes leading to executive selection, nomination, and appointment. And whereas initially these commitments were perhaps confined largely to the components of political persuasion and geography, the passing parade of the century in which we live has witnessed the insistent adoption and adaptation of such additional expectations and requirements as contemporarily inform the "representation" of race, gender, religion, geography, and perhaps even age. Whatever the Constitution's framers' ascertainable intentions may have been, the notion of the entitlement to a "peer model" has become all but pervasive in judicial staffing today. Personally, I regard it as of dubious wisdom and, in fact, regrettable.

If, as the great Holmes insisted so warmly, a page of history is truly worth more than a volume of logic, one might have little difficulty in arriving at history's verdict on the conundrum of "representativeness" in the appointment process. The past, however, is prologue as well as history. It may thus be argued with some cogency that the "equitable components" enumerated above operate currently in a setting of our democratic polity that is naturally quite at variance with that of the late eighteenth century—in moral, philosophical, and political terms. It is a setting that would be demonstrably puzzling or foreign to the Founding Fathers, whose fledgling republic enjoyed a degree of homogeneity never again to be equaled in this land's ensuing history. Nonetheless, even granting the imperatives of the polity's dramatic transformation, one may well still pose the troubling question that underlies these painful ruminations, namely: Is the nation, is the citizenry, served better, served more appropriately, if "representativeness" is rendered a prolegomenon for judicial selection, nomination, and appointment?

The attempted answer has evoked lively, often bitter, debate for close to half-a-century now, reaching a crescendo during the past generation. [My dear old teacher and friend, Dumas Malone—who, alas, died on Christmas 1986, one month prior to his 95th birthday, told me that Mr. Jefferson's definition of "generation" encompassed 19 or 20 years. Needless to say that I would never challenge Professor Malone and assuredly not on matters Jeffersonian!] I suspect that the verdict is in: if something can be "more or less" *RES JUDICATA*, it is obvious that the political branches have embraced "representativeness." That the pages of history demonstrate beyond any shadow of a doubt that the Founding Fathers did not ponder the issue does not necessarily determine its wisdom or desirability. But it is on those frontiers that an opinion opting for the sole criterion of merit as the irreducible imperative basic threshold requirement may be respectfully submitted, joined to the plea cum conviction that any "plus" considerations in behalf of "representativeness" must be wholly dependent upon the demonstrable presence of individual merit at the threshold.

## III.

The concept, the phenomenon, of merit unfortunately defies universal definition; it is neither axiom nor theorem. It may even lie entirely in the eye and mind of the beholder, but it need not do so. It is possible to suggest a merit model, and I should like to do so, eschewing any claim to originality. An octet, the model comprises the following self-evident components (in no particular order of significance):

One: demonstrated judicial temperament
Two: professional expertise and competence
Three: absolute personal as well as professional integrity
Four: an able, agile, lucid mind
Five: appropriate professional educational background or training
Six: the ability to communicate clearly, both orally and in writing, and especially the latter
Seven: resolute fair-mindedness
Eight: a solid understanding of the proper judicial role of judges under our Constitution

Not only do these constitute achievable components, but the history of our Supreme Court has demonstrated their presence amply. If the Holmesian tongue-in-cheek aphorism that the job of a jurist requires a "combination of Justinian, Jesus Christ, and John Marshall" may not always have been attainable, it is apposite to note that with one possible exception even that trio may not have been perfect! If political party affiliation has almost always played a role, well, there are but nine positions on the highest bench, and there are unquestionably just as many qualified Republicans as there are qualified Democrats, and as many qualified Democrats as there are qualified Republicans among our America's (all-too-many) 700,000 lawyers. Nor is there any gainsaying a nominator's resolve to select a nominee with whom he is ideologically and jurisprudentially comfortable. You would, and I would, act similarly, always assuming the presence of threshold merit.

Of course, merit may also be expressed quite differently as it was, for example, by Bruce E. Fein, a top Justice Department official in the early days of the Reagan Administration. He set forth five more subjective requirements for the selection of a Supreme Court Justice, requirements that seek merit yet concurrently also present a clarion call for jurisprudential commitments. His quintet comprised:

[1.] An understanding that the Supreme Court is not the nation's moral conscience, does not monopolize the nation's concern for minority interests and is not infallible . . . [2.] A conviction that the express language of the Constitution and intent of the framers are the only legitimate guides to constitutional interpretation . . . [3.] An understanding of the constitutional scheme of federalism; a tolerance of divergent policies among the 50 states . . . [4.] Knowledge of the network of nonjudicial mechanisms that safeguard against abuse of government power . . . [and 5.] A recognition that the paramount federal judicial role is to decide on concrete cases, not gratuitously to pronounce on the constitutionality of action taken by Congress, the President, or the states.

While there has been a trickle increase in biographical studies of Supreme Court Justices, my recent involvement in researching just what has been done must render the regrettable judgment of "not nearly enough." There are many good reasons that account for that fact, among them the delicate and difficult problem of the existence and availability of the papers of Justices, plus the dearth of biographical craftsmen of the stature of Princeton's Professor Emeritus Alpheus Thomas Mason. Yet there are enough data to permit an annotated catalog of the major historically ascertainable decisional reasons or motivations for the presidential selection of members of the bench. In rendering such judgments, one must acknowledge concurrently that only the incumbent president really knows why he either selected a nominee to the Court or gave the nod to others, in effect, to select for him.

History does demonstrate, however, that an identifiable quartet of such reasons or motivations may be safely pinpointed to have governed the selection process—a quartet that, were I a quantifier or "behavioralist," might well lend itself to at least a measure of statistical proof. That quartet of criteria is: (1) objective merit, (2) personal and political friendship, (3) balancing "representation" on the Court, and (4) "real" political and ideological compatibility. Obviously, more than just one of these factors was present in most of the nominations, and in some all four were. Yet it is not at all impossible to point to one as the overriding one.

At any rate, as president after president has found out, without any particular degree of amusement, if there is anything certain about his nominees' on-bench performance in jurisprudential terms, it is that it is hardly predictable with accuracy, let alone certainty—which, to a very considerable degree, is—arguably—a comforting fact of the judicial process. "You shoot an arrow into a far-distant future," wrote Yale University's famed constitutional scholar, Alexander M. Bickel, not long before his untimely death in 1974, "when you appoint a justice and not the man himself can tell you what he will think about some of the problems he will face. "

That is, of course, why such wise politicians as that "All-American Boy President," Theodore Roosevelt, in a famed exchange with Massachusetts Republican United States Senator Henry Cabot Lodge regarding the potential candidacy of Democrat Horace H. Lurton in 1906, wrote his objecting fellow-Republican that "the nominal politics of the man has nothing to do with his actions on the bench. His real politics are all important." And "T. R." lauded Mr. Lurton's position on sundry policies "in which you and I believe." Lodge concurred in substance, but replied that he saw no reason "why Republicans cannot be found who hold these opinions as well as Democrats." Insistently, he urged the appointment of the incumbent Attorney General, Will H. Moody, whom T. R. then sent to the Court.

This raises the already alluded-to, and certainly clearly implied, question of "court-packing." Whether in fact presidents can really pack the Court is a *quaere* that is as intriguing as it is constantly recurring.

In the public eye, court-packing has been most closely associated with President Franklin D. Roosevelt. Having had not a single opportunity to fill a Supreme Court vacancy in his first term (1933–37), and seeing his domestic programs consistently battered by the Court, the frustrated president attempted to get his way all at once. His "Court-packing bill," however, died a deserved death in the Senate by being recommitted in 1937.

It is of course not surprising that court-packing and the name of Franklin D. Roosevelt have become synonymous. Yet even such popular presidential heroes as Jefferson, Jackson, and Lincoln followed similar courses of action in the face of what they considered "judicial intransigence and defiance." Their approach was not as radical as "F.D.R.," but they very likely would have been sympathetic to his efforts. President George Washington, though broadly regarded as far removed from "politics," in fact remains the champion "court-packer" to date. He had insisted that his fourteen nominees to the Court meet a veritable *smorgasbord* of qualifications. There were seven, to be exact, and he adhered to them religiously: (1) support and advocacy of the Constitution; (2) distinguished service in the Revolution; (3) active participation in the political life of state or nation; (4) prior judicial experience on lower tribunals; (5) either a "favorable reputation with his fellows," or personal ties with Washington himself; (6) geographic "suitability"; and (7) "love of our country." Of these criteria, evidently the most important to him was advocacy of the principles of the Constitution—and the more outspoken the better. Perhaps more than many of his contemporaries he recognized the potential strength and influence of the judicial branch, keenly sensing the role it would be called on to play in spelling out constitutional basics and penumbras. In letters of commission to his initial six nominees to the fledgling nation's first Supreme Court in September and October of 1789, he wrote: "The Judicial System is the chief Pillar upon which our national Government must rest." That "Pillar" needed strong men—proponents of the Federalist-philosophy of government. Indeed, seven of those the president sent to the bench had been participants in the Constitutional Convention of 1787. He knew most, if not all, of his appointees intimately.

In point of fact, every president who has made nominations to the Supreme Court has been guilty of court-packing in some measure. You would do so if you were in that exalted position and so would I. It is entirely understandable that a president will choose those who will share his own philosophy of government and politics, at least to the extent of giving him a sympathetic hearing. Theodore Roosevelt, for example, in discussing the above-described potential candidacy of Horace H. Lurton with Henry Cabot Lodge, put the issue well:

> The nominal politics of the man has nothing to do with his actions on the bench. His real politics are all important. . . . He is right on the Negro question; he is right on the power of the federal government; he is right on the Insular business; he is right about corporations, and he is right about labor.
>
> On every question that would come before the bench, he has so far shown himself to be in much closer touch with the policies in which you and I believe than even [Associate Justice Edward D.] White because he has been right about corporations where White has been wrong.

Lodge concurred in substance, but he replied that he could see no reason "why Republicans cannot be found who hold those opinions as well as Democrats." Consequently, he strongly urged the candidacy of a Republican, whom T. R. then duly nominated—the aforementioned William H. Moody, Attorney General of Massachusetts.

## IV.

Thus, concern with a nominee's *real* politics is a fundamental issue, and examples abound. It prompted Republican Taft to give half of his six appointments to Democrats who were kindred souls, Republican Nixon to appoint Democrat Powell, Democrat Roosevelt to promote Republican Stone, and Democrat Truman to appoint Republican Burton—to mention just a few examples in point. Yet there is no guarantee that what a president perceives as real politics will not fade into a mirage. Hence Charles Warren, eminent chronicler of the Court, observed quite properly that, "nothing is more striking in the history of the Court than the manner in which the hopes of those who expected a judge to follow the political views of the President appointing him are disappointed." Few have felt the truth of that statement more keenly than Teddy Roosevelt did with Oliver Wendell Holmes, Jr., whose early "anti-administration" opinions in antitrust cases (notably in *Northern Securities v.*

*United States*) were entirely unexpected. A bare 5:4 majority in that 1904 case upheld the government's order, under the Sherman Anti-Trust Act, dissolving the Northern Securities Company, brainchild of E. H. Harriman and J. J. Hill, the wealthy and powerful owners of competing railroads who had organized the company in order to secure a terminal line into Chicago. Roosevelt had won that important litigation, but he was furious about his recent appointee's "anti-anti-trust" vote in the case. He stormed: "I could carve out of a banana a judge with more backbone than that!" Holmes reportedly merely smiled when told about the president's remark, referred to him as "a shallow intellect," and noted his intention to "call the shots as I see them in terms of the legal and constitutional setting." Later, during "T. R.'s " second term of office (1905–09), Holmes expressed his sentiments to a labor leader at a White House dinner: "What you want is favor, not justice. But when I am on my job, I don't give a damn what you or Mr. Roosevelt want. "

James Madison, having refused to heed his political mentor, Thomas Jefferson, was similarly chagrined with his appointment of Justice Joseph Story. Jefferson had warned him that Story was an inveterate Tory who would become a rabid supporter of Chief Justice Marshall, and he was right: Story not only instantly joined Marshall's approach to constitutional adjudication and interpretation, but he even out-Marshalled Marshall in his nationalism. Perhaps even more chagrined—although he could not have been utterly surprised—was Woodrow Wilson when his appointee James C. McReynolds proved himself at once to be the antithesis of almost everything his nominator stood for and believed in.

More recently, Harry Truman observed that "packing the Supreme Court simply can't be done. . . . I've tried and it won't work. . . . Whenever you put a man on the Supreme Court he ceases to be your friend. I'm sure of that. Lord knows I've tried!" And he had! But not only did he fail to be pleased in his expectations, he appointed a group of four that would not make the list of "greats" or "near greats" on any of the several formal ratings or rankings of Supreme Court Justices: Burton, Vinson, Clark, and Minton. Ironically, Truman reserved his most bitter attack because of "nonsupport" for the best of the four, his one-time Attorney General, Tom C. Clark. The president was furious with Clark for what he viewed as Clark's "anti-Truman" vote in the *Steel Seizure Case* of 1952. There, in a carefully crafted concurring opinion, Clark joined five other colleagues in disallowing Truman's seizure of the struck steel mills; all six, in diverse compass, objected to executive usurpation of legislative authority in the presence of ascertainable congressional intent contrary to the president's wishes. Truman was not amused; in fact, he was livid, calling Clark "[t]hat damn fool from Texas" and "my biggest mistake," adding "well, it isn't so much that he is a bad man. It's just that he is such a dumb son of a bitch. He's about the dumbest man I think I have ever run across." Clark was hurt, but the deep personal friendship between the two men continued, their closeness apparently unaffected.

The story of President Dwight D. Eisenhower's disenchantment with two of his five appointees, Chief Justice Earl Warren and Associate Justice William J. Brennan, Jr., is well known. Sparring with reports aboard Air Force One on one of his last days in office, Ike was asked whether he had ever committed any serious mistakes in office. "Oh, sure," he replied. "Yes, Mr. President," came the rejoinder, "but did you ever make any 'beauts,' Sir?" "Yep," Ike intoned, "and they are both on the Supreme Court! . . . Biggest damn-fooled mistake I ever made." His reference was to the two aforementioned jurists.

Eisenhower's successor, Richard M. Nixon, was initially delighted with the voting pattern of the second of his four appointees, Associate Justice Harry Blackmun, whom the press soon derisively dubbed "the Minnesota twin," for he was so frequently recorded on the same side as his old friend and fellow-Minnesotan, Chief Justice Warren Burger. But gradually—or, indeed, not-so-gradually—Blackmun began to assert his independence and commenced a steady journey to the "liberal" or "left" side of the Court, where he became a now usually predictable ally—except in certain criminal justice cases—of Justices Brennan and Marshall, and, later, of Stevens. In effect Blackmun moved from a 90 percent agreement with Burger in his first three years on the Court to a 70 percent agreement with Brennan thereafter. Nixon filled the air with expletives after the controversial Blackmun-authored opinion in the 1973 *Abortion Cases of Roe v. Wade* and *Doe v. Bolton*. Nixon had been only slightly less disenchanted with Justice Lewis F. Powell, Jr.'s surprise authorship, for his unanimous brethren, in *United States v. United States District Court for the Eastern District of Michigan* in 1972, just shortly after the Virginia brahmin had joined the Court. As a private citizen Powell had publicly *supported* the Nixon Administration's claim of constitutional authority for wire-tapping of radical domestic groups *without* a warrant; yet when the issue reached the Court, the Powell opinion declared that contention and practice to be an *unconstitutional* invasion of Fourth Amendment guarantees as well as being unauthorized under the applicable federal law, as enacted by Congress. And, of course, Mr. Nixon did not garner a single supportive vote in the Court's unanimous ruling against him in *United States v. Nixon*, also known as the Nixon Tapes Case of 1974.

## V.

Well, then, can our chief executives really pack the Court? The tentative, perhaps equivocal, answer I suggest is both "yes" and "no." To the extent that a president can reliably ascertain one of his nominees' "real politics," to re-utilize that fortunate Theodore Roosevelt–Henry Cabot Lodge terminology, the answer is affirmative. Examples are legion—not perhaps with 100 percent certainty (what is?), yet with a comfortable degree of majoritarian reliability. "F. D. R." needed to be certain of a person who would supply a "safe" vote for his New Deal program when he at last gained a vacancy in 1937: He took no chances, whatsoever, with Senator Hugo Lafayette Black of Alabama. Nor did he with William O. Douglas. Ike's selection of New York's patrician John Marshall Harlan was similarly safe. So were Lyndon B. Johnson's of Thurgood Marshall and of Arthur Goldberg. So were Richard Nixon's of Warren Burger and William Rehnquist. With some qualifications, so seems to have been President Ronald Reagan's of Sandra Day O'Connor—although she has manifested some interesting, and increasingly numerous, departures from the proverbial reservation. Yet perplexing, indeed, to him must be the intriguing maverick record of Antonin Scalia, who quickly demonstrated that he is far from being an individual who is in the confidently predicted jurisprudentially conservative bag! Nothing is certain, obviously, and examples of assertions of judicial independence thus abound even among those who, based on their past record, would appear to be categorizable as generally safe. Still, as a general rule, most, albeit not all—"T. R." was very unhappy with his, save for Moody—presidents have had reason to be more or less satisfied. To at least some degree Court-packing is plausible, even if only marginally. Yet the presence of such major "anti-nominator" on-Court stances as, for example, Eisenhower's appointees Warren and Brennan; Nixon's Blackmun; Madison's Story; Wilson's McReynolds; and, it is arguably fair to conjecture, Reagan's Scalia, tempers . . . that earlier judgment. Tempers, yes, but, again arguably, in a clear majority of these admittedly extreme "anti-nominator" instances, more careful, more reflective, more assiduous pre-nomination research would have seeded considerable doubt and might have raised warning flags on the nomination's political safeness or wisdom: Ike had been severally alerted to Warren's patent progressivism; Madison's mentor, Thomas Jefferson, had cautioned him repeatedly that Story would "out-Marshall" Marshall—and he assuredly did; Wilson had been amply and insistently warned against McReynold's reactionary tendencies and bigotry. The more intriguing, and far less clear instances, of attempted court-packing having gone awry, on the other hand, are the very considerable number of instances in which the yeasty independence of a justice's on-bench existence produces the kind of unpredictable and nominator-maddening votes that have been cast by many a Justice, for example, the first John Marshall Harlan, Holmes, Reed, Frankfurter, White, Powell, Stevens, and Scalia.

It is a long and often obstacle-strewn path between the nomination of a jurist and the latter in decisional stance. Hence, future presidents may be well advised to heed the admonition of Zechariah Chafee, Harvard's famed expert on the judicial process, who contended that to forecast the behavior of a future jurist it is wiser to consider the books in his or her library than the list of clients in the candidate's office. That may or may not serve as a yardstick. Of course, it is not quite so simple. Yet there is indeed a considerable element of unpredictability in the judicial appointing process, and so be it. To the often heard, "Does a person become any different when he puts on a gown?" Justice Frankfurter's sharp retort was always, "If he is any good, he does!" To reiterate the words of Alexander M. Bickel, "You shoot an arrow into a far-distant future when you appoint a Justice and not the man himself can tell you what he will think about some of the problems that he will face." And late in 1969, reflecting on his sixteen years as Chief Justice of the United States, Earl Warren pointed out that he, for one, did not "see how a man could be on the Court and not change his views substantially over a period of years . . . for change you must if you are to do your duty on the Supreme Court." It is a duty that, in many ways, represents the most hallowed in the governmental process of the United States.

Whatever one's view of the achievements of the several jurists I have mentioned in these ruminations, many merit our affection and admiration. Their numbers testify to the rich mine of giants that have served so remarkably well on the Court in its now almost two centuries of life. They provide proof positive of promises fulfilled and achievements rendered. Indeed, notwithstanding the often tiresome, and not infrequently self-serving—albeit exasperating—sniping that has characterized the Court's existence, sniping that has regrettably although not surprisingly, emanated most loudly from prestigious centers of learning located near bodies of water on both the East and West coasts, it has, I submit with conviction, truly been, in James Madison's words, a "bench happily filled." His wish cum plea, expressed in 1787, has stood the test of time admirably. One should never close, be it a written or vocalized statement, by quoting from someone else. But I hope you will forgive my doing so with a touching tribute to one of those giants who graced the Court, Benjamin Nathan Cardozo. It came from the pen of his friend and fellow supreme judicial stylist and craftsman, Learned Hand, who movingly eulogized the gentle spirit shortly after his death in 1938, concluding:

> In this America of ours where the passion for publicity is a disease, and where swarms of foolish, tawdry moths dash with rapture into its consuming fire, it was a rare good fortune that brought to such eminence a man so reserved, so unassuming, so retiring, so gracious to high and low, and so

> serene. He is gone, and while the west is still lighted with his radiance, it is well for us to pause and take count of our own coarser selves. He had a lesson to teach us if we care to stop and learn; a lesson at variance with most that we practice, and much that we profess.

* * *

*Louis Henkin.* Have you studied the role of the Senate in the same way? If the President can pack, can the Senate pack? Or pack backwards?

*Henry Abraham.* Along with others, I have indeed studied the Senate's role. Contrary to Mr. Nixon's assertions, the Senate cannot "pack" the Court; but it can prevent nominees from mounting it. To be precise, it has done so 27 times: 23 in the last century, four in this. Again, contrary to Nixon's angry contentions in 1969–70, the Senate has every right to reject on ideological grounds if it wants to do so. As the constitutional partner it is clearly entitled to say "no" to a nominee, yet it does not have the right to carry on in the mindless fashion that it sometimes does. I think, for example, that last summer's Senatorial performance vis-à-vis Chief Justice-designate Rehnquist was inexcusably hostile and protracted. No wonder that Antonin Scalia was asked practically no questions—the senators were exhausted by the time they turned to him!

# Symposium on the Genius of the United States Constitution

## *Remarks*

**ARTHUR S. LINK**

*George Henry Davis '86 Professor of American History; Editor,* The Papers of Woodrow Wilson

When the Committee on Meetings asked me to organize a symposium celebrating the bicentennial of the Constitution, I at once thought of a general theme—"The Genius of the Constitution"—because the questions that it evokes have long intrigued me. Like most students of American history who came to adulthood during the high tide of progressivism during the Great Depression and The New Deal, I was no worshiper of the Founding Fathers. They were, after all, as Charles A. Beard had told us in *An Economic Interpretation of the Constitution*, simply legitimating and protecting their own economic self-interests in imposing the Constitution upon an electorate that was either reluctant, beguiled, or bedazzled to accept it. And yet I had, even then, serious doubts about the validity of a single interpretation. Historical scholarship since about 1950 on the background and origins of the Constitution has forced me and most of my contemporaries to bring old, nagging questions to the fronts of our minds. And this scholarly work, combined with the experience of living through a period when the very notion of the viability of constitutional government was gravely challenged, has converted doubts about Beard's simplistic reductionism into new certainties about the genius and grandeur of the framers of 1787.

Let us frankly say what we now believe—that Gladstone was not far from the mark when he said that the Constitution is the most remarkable document ever struck off by the mind of man at a given moment. That may be true, but questions still call out for answers. How was it possible for a country, not yet a nation, of three and a half million people to call forth a body of men unparalleled in history for learning, wisdom, and great good sense, who then, in a remarkably short time, produced a frame of national government that has survived for these two hundred years? Not only has it survived, but it has also proved capable of meeting unbelievable demands upon it occasioned by the most portentous challenges and changes since the dawn of the modern era. Great genius obviously inheres in a document that produced that kind of frame of government. But how can we unlock the secrets of this genius, how disclose them?

To find the answers, I turned to the four authorities whose work makes up the following part of this volume. Choosing them was an easy task, because they are among the brightest and the best of a generation of scholars who have turned Beard on his head and revolutionized our knowledge and understanding of the motives, objectives, and accomplishments of the Founding Fathers. They unlock the secrets of the genius of the Constitution from different angles and perspectives, to be sure, but their commentaries constitute a harmonious testimony. I have resisted the temptation to repeat what they have so wisely said, for the excitement of discovering the riches of their chapters belongs to the readers of this volume. However, on behalf of the American Philosophical Society, it is my privilege to thank them sincerely for some of the liveliest and most insightful commentaries on the Constitution ever written.

# *A More Perfect Union*

**GARRY WILLS**

*Henry R. Luce Professor of American Culture and Public Policy, Northwestern University*

Say "checks," in constitutionspeak, and you almost have to say "balances"—though what, if anything, the second adds to the first is rarely specified. The unit is an emphatic, like the prefix in "co-equal" with *its* inevitable partner, "branches." How did the canonical double billing of "checks and balances" arise? Not from the Constitution, which knows the terms neither singly nor in conjunction. But if "check" or "balance" does not occur in the text, neither does "separation of powers," nor "federalism," nor "branches" of any sort (co-equal or merely equal). "Equal" first turns up in the Fourteenth Amendment, where it refers to the individual's protection under law, not to parts of government. We all need words, for saying what the Constitution is about, that the Constitution did not require.

But never mind. We already know what that document means to say, even if it never quite manages to say it. We have been let in on its secret before it begins to speak. We know about its fear of power, its jealousy of office, its distrust of human nature. These have been affirmed for us by the best authorities. Arthur Lovejoy, seeking an archetypal expression of the low view of human nature, found the Constitution apt to his purpose. It accomplishes so much because its authors expected so little from their fellow beings.

> The ablest members of the Constitutional Convention were well aware that their task—unlike that of the Continental Congress of 1776—was not to lay down abstract principles of political philosophy, not to rest the system they were constructing simply upon theorems about the "natural rights" of men or of States, though they postulated such rights. Their problem was not chiefly one of political ethics but of practical psychology, a need not so much to preach to Americans about what they ought to do, as to

> predict successfully what they would do, supposing certain governmental mechanisms were (or were not) established.[1]

They settled, that is, for less highfalutin ideals than the Declaration of Independence had brandished. The framers had to make do with the imperfect instruments of a workaday world. Walter Bagehot went further, and said the whole of the Constitution is good precisely because every one of its parts is bad. Its effectiveness is derived from accumulating defects. It is, in his words, "a government [so] constructed in which its evil tendencies exactly check, balance, and destroy one another—in which a good whole is constructed not simply in spite of but by means of the contrasting defects of the constituent parts."[2] Actually, I cheat a bit in that citation. Bagehot was describing the mythical British Constitution, which so pleased Montesquieu. But some Americans have made their document even more gleefully dependent on human frailty, enough to please a Mandeville as well as a Montesquieu.

Thus, though the Constitution is chronologically the product of the American Enlightenment, it seems profoundly at odds with the spirit of the European Enlightenment. That movement, we have been led to suppose, expressed a certain optimism about the possibility of progress, of improvement, of a human capacity for higher achievements. But the Constitution settled for less, for a certain poise or stasis, a balance that was permitted to block the energies of progressive actions so long as that prevented abuses of energy for tyrannical ends. The Enlightenment invented instruments of efficient control, based on people's inventive genius. The Constitution is praised for its inefficiency, its wonderful contrivances for repeatedly stalling, its propensity for getting nowhere or actually backing up, its thwarting of ambitious talents.

In short, the Constitution is practical and down to earth because it has no touch with the snappy idealisms of the Enlightened, who indulged in dreams of human perfectibility. Here, for instance, is the kind of talk we do not expect to hear around the drafting convention in Philadelphia: "Such is the order of Providence with regard to society [that] it is in a progressive state, moving on towards perfection." Good Enlightenment talk, that. But bad constitutional commentary. Here is another effusion from the same source:

> We may infer that the law of nature, so immutable in its principles, will be progressive in its operations and effects. Indeed, the same immutable

[1] Arthur O. Lovejoy, *Reflections on Human Nature* (Johns Hopkins University, 1961), 46–47.
[2] Walter Bagehot, *The English Constitution*, 1872 edition (Oxford: Oxford University, 1974), 2.

> principles will direct this progression. In every period of his existence, the law, which the divine wisdom has approved for man, will not only be fitted, to the contemporary degree, but will be calculated to produce, in future, a still higher degree of perfection.

That sounds like Jefferson's view that our descendants must be as much advanced over us as we are over our ancestors—and his spirit was notoriously absent from Philadelphia during the drafting sessions.

Let me keep quoting our Enlightenment source, so distant from the framers' hard-nosed realism (or tragic pessimism):

> A progressive state is necessary to the happiness and perfection of man. Whatever attainments are already reached, attainments still higher shall be pursued. Let us, therefore, strive with noble emulation. Let us suppose we have done nothing while anything yet remains to be done. Let us with fervent zeal press forward, and make unceasing advances in everything that can support, improve, refine, or embellish society.

A generous program, indeed, one going far beyond the modest hopes of the framers as those are presented by the Lovejoys, who tell us how good our Constitution is in its reliance on the bad propensities of man. We may well feel it is a *misleading* accident of chronology that made the Constitution appear in the late eighteenth century, when other parts of the world were flirting with the giddier emotions of the Enlightenment.

But lest we push too definitively to that judgment, I must let you in on a secret about all those passages I have just quoted concerning human progress and social perfection. They are all taken from the first public exposition of the new Constitution as a legal system; and they were written by a man well qualified to know what went into the making of the Constitution—he was a principal framer himself, and the principal defender of the ratification period, and the re-drafter of the Pennsylvania Constitution to conform to the spirit of the federal document, and an authorized interpreter of the Constitution as one of the original Supreme Court justices. The words I have been quoting—and there are many more in the same vein—are from James Wilson's *Law Lectures* of 1790, designed to be the Blackstone for a more liberal system of law than England ever knew.[3] Wilson went so far as to argue that Henry IV's plan for Europe's perpetual peace, designed by one "too enlightened for the age in which he lived," has come to fulfillment in the American system, which, if

---

[3] *The Works of James Wilson*, edited by Robert Green McCloskey (Harvard University, 1967). The passages cited are from 84, 147, 779. See also 260, 444.

imitated, could procure the happiness of mankind in general.[4] Heady stuff, and not the language we expect to hear about our ruling document.

But remember what are the things we expect to hear from the Constitution and never do—any mention of checks, balances, separation, of limits, federalism, or the other famous dampers on government power. We are not told about executive or legislative checks, but about the executive power, the legislative powers. The Constitution is an act of *empowerment*, a grant of powers felt to be scarcely large enough to many of the time. The powers were meant to reach large goals—to establish justice, insure domestic tranquility, promote the general welfare. But the proudest goal comes first, and seems so bold that it might as well be written in invisible ink for all the attention it normally gets. What holds primacy of place in the work of the framers? It was placed where, it would seem, we could not miss it: "We the People of the United States, in order to form *a more perfect* Union."

That is the direct answer to the charge the framers had given themselves at the outset. They went into committee of the whole with the commission "to consider of the state of the American Union"[5]—and their direct report was that a more perfect union was needed. This in a document that is supposed to avoid all truck with notions of human perfectibility!

What, in such a context, could a perfect union mean, much less a *more* perfect one? Where Aristotle had set government the task of reaching its own *telos*, of becoming perfected (*telestheisa*), a perfect government was one with all its *parts*, its *moria* in Greek.[6] (He wrote a whole treatise on the *moria* of animals, those limbs without which they were defective.) A perfect body had a similar sense in obstetric circles for centuries—one with all its toes and ears and things. Plato's *Republic* had been defective, Aristotle claimed, for lack of just such essential appendages. It sought a false simplicity reducing harmony to monotone.[7] A government must have all the organs necessary to its functions. Only thus does it have the *autarkeia* of a classical *polis*.

Now one of the things that had been borne in on American political thinkers and activists during the 1780s was that, in their cluster of revolutionary governments, adopted in ragged sequence during the war, the Americans

---

[4] Ibid., 261.

[5] Journal of the Federal Convention, 29 May 1787, in Max Farrand, *The Records of the Federal Convention of 1787* (Yale University, 1966), 1: 16.

[6] *Aristotelis Politica*, edited by W. D. Ross (Oxford, 1952), 3 (1252b33).

[7] Ibid., 35 (1263b34–35).

nowhere had a perfect government. They had a collection of fourteen imperfect, incomplete governments, none of them truly sovereign or self-sufficient. It is true that the thirteen constituted states of the confederacy claimed, in Article II, that they retained entire sovereignty. But in fact no one state could form an alliance or go to war without the permission of the others; and a state that found itself in a minority could be forced into a war it did not, singly, choose. States whose diplomatic powers are maimed or nonexistent could hardly be called "sovereign." But the confederate Congress formed by the Articles was also incomplete, even more hampered and hedged about than the states it was supposed to preside over. It was an anomalous thing, given largely executive duties (conducting the Revolutionary War and the postrevolutionary diplomacy) without having any defined executive body. It had a legislative structure with little or no power to vindicate its laws either by force or by adjudication. This anomaly was often noted. Even Thomas Burke of North Carolina, the very man who had forced the insertion of the state sovereignty clause into the Articles, later said that Congress could not function because it was "a deliberating executive assembly."[8] John Adams called it "not a legislative assembly, not a representative assembly, but only a diplomatic assembly."[9] As such, it could not execute for deliberating, and it could not deliberate for executing.

The situation was so desperate that Congress began dividing itself, against the mandate of the Articles, into committees that became a de facto executive for enacting policies day by day without reference back to the present body of Congress. There was even an attempt to bring in unelected committeemen as executors, since Congressmen found it impossible to be present both in Congress and in the committees when those bodies were sitting concurrently.[10]

The Congress did not entirely lack a judicial function, but it lacked a sitting body to discharge that function. When Congress was asked, according to the provision of Article IX, to superintend the Trenton trial of 1782, establishing jurisdiction over the Wyoming territory, a cumbrous ad hoc machinery had to be built up, and it proved so unwieldy in operation and so unsatisfactory in result that it guaranteed the process would never be tried again.[11] Instead, Congress took directly on itself the settling of territorial claims and the setting

---

[8] Jack N. Rakove, *The Beginnings of National Politics: An Interpretive History of the Continental Congress* (Knopf, 1979), 202.

[9] Ibid., 175.

[10] Ibid., 199–203.

[11] Peter S. Onuf, *The Origins of the Federal Republic: Jurisdictional Controversies in the United States, 1775–1787* (University of Pennsylvania, 1983), 57–61.

up of territorial governments—in the Northwest Ordinances of 1784 and 1787, both of which were probably unconstitutional at the time of their passage, but necessary expedients for government without the minimum of functioning parts.[12]

How address this continuing, worsening problem? Obviously by *adding* parts to the confederation government, by perfecting the union, by escaping the simplicity that was a flaw. If we come at the drafting of the Constitution from this direction, as the framers themselves did, we see a reason for the separation of power other than the one that springs to mind repeatedly when later commentators look at the document. These commentators assume there can be no other reason to separate power than to divide the federal responsibilities, weaken its components, keep one or the other from prevailing, dilute the strength of government itself. That was not the vantage point from which the framers looked at the matter. They already had one predominant department of government—the Continental Congress—and far from tyrannizing; it was debilitated by *its singleness*. It was a limbless trunk. It needed separate powers as an extension of its powers, a perfection of its union. It would become one by becoming many, the Aristotelian paradox of government. The new departments of government added to the *capacities* of the government. A sitting body of judges is more efficient than a panel assembled anew for each case. The age of Enlightenment is also the period that celebrated the division of labor as an efficiency measure. Hume derived government itself from a division of labor—the best hunters hunt full time, the best planners plan, the best mediators mediate, and a simple tribal society gradually articulates itself into a civilized polity with its specialized branches.

We know that Madison wanted greater efficiency in the national government. Indeed, he left Philadelphia disappointed that he had not prevailed on what he considered an essential power, that of the national government to veto state laws and enforce the veto by arms. It cannot have been his principal aim, in separating power, to make the government even more inefficient, more deadlocked, more self-checking, than the Continental Congress. Perfecting the union did not mean lopping off limbs or organs but adding them on. It invented useful new parts of government. In fact, much of the spirit of the document is expressed in an often neglected clause in the first Article, just another item in the lost list of empowerments, but the *only* one to have its own little preamble where the infinitive does not merely specify the act to be

---

[12] Ibid., 169–71.

undertaken but sets a goal for the action that is added by a prepositional phrase. We have a run of things that Congress has power to do—

1. —to coin money . . .
2. —to provide for the punishment of counterfeiting . . .
3. —to establish post offices. . . .

And then:

> —*to promote the progress of science and useful arts*, by securing for limited times to authors and inventors the exclusive right to their respective writings and discoveries. . . .

That was an appropriate power to be granted by a body in which Benjamin Franklin was sitting. Or for what matter, one presided over by George Washington. Those were the two men, along with David Rittenhouse, whose names Thomas Jefferson used to prove that America was as enlightened as Europe. No wonder this country produced that Enlightenment document, the Constitution.

* * *

*John Wheeler*. Kurt Gödel being a member of this Society wanted also to become a citizen of the United States and qualified by residence in this country. He had studied the Constitution to which he would have to take his allegiance, but in the end he gave it up because it was logically inconsistent.*

*Garry Wills*. I hate to disagree with so eminent an authority as Gödel, but I find that the Constitution *is* logical, is *not* self-cancelling. Not only are there no checks and balances mentioned, there is no permanent stasis aimed at in the document. The legislature necessarily predominates as Madison said in #51. It has the power to restructure the other two branches. The other two branches cannot dissolve the legislature or dismiss a single member. Congress has the right to rewrite a Constitution in conjunction with the states. Neither of the other two has that. It has *all* legislative powers; it can reconstruct the executive branch, as we've seen with the special prosecutor. It can reconstruct the judicial branch; it can impeach any member of the other two branches, any officer of the United States. So, there is a great deal of logic, there is a separation of powers, but by no means a co-equal or self-cancelling or contradictory structure. And much of that language of co-equal branches, checks and balances, was used primarily as an attack upon the Constitution in the ratifying period, calling for things that were not in the Constitution. If you look at the ratifying conventions in the various states, the people who talk most about checks and balances are the opponents of the Constitution, who say they are not there. And they are right. They are not.

*[Editorial comment: Herman H. Goldstine]

Let me try to finish the history of Gödel's citizenship. In point of fact, he did become a U.S. citizen; and this is the story as I heard it from Oskar Morganstern in Princeton. It is perfectly true that Gödel thought he had found a logical contradiction in the Constitution of the United States, and that he could therefore not subscribe to it. Von Neumann, however, by some sort of argument or other, convinced him that it was not contradictory, and that in fact the system was contradiction free. Gödel thereupon decided to become a citizen and asked Albert Einstein and Oskar Morganstern to be his sponsors in the Federal District Court in Trenton.

He appeared there one day with these two sponsors before a federal judge who was so awed and impressed by Einstein's presence that he barely noticed Gödel's existence. He talked at great length with Einstein about many topics, including at the end, Nazi atrocities, and the terrible things that happened in Germany under Hitler. The judge, suddenly remembering that Gödel was there to be naturalized, turned to him and said, "Those things couldn't happen here in the United States, could they, Professor Gödel?" Whereupon, Gödel, suddenly remembering some of his doubts about the Constitution, said, "Let me tell you, Your Honor, perhaps they could." Whereupon, both Einstein and Morganstern dug their elbows into his ribs and told him to say, "No, it couldn't happen," which he did. Thereupon he became an American citizen.

*Speaker unknown.* Would it be correct to say that there was a skeptical strain in the Enlightenment and that your picture of the Enlightenment is essentially the Condorcet version, but there was also Voltairian?

*Garry Wills.* Yes. It is silly to type any one person and especially any one age as simply and solely optimistic, simply and solely pessimistic. Even in the skeptical and questioning side of the Enlightenment, there was, in Hume, a reliance on the instincts of morality, which made him a very conservative politician; and there was, in Voltaire, a trust in the sensibility of mankind that made him think tearful tragedies would convert people where pure reason would not. So he spent most of his time writing tragedies nobody reads anymore. We tend to read rather his skeptical attacks on superstition. It might be more rewarding to read his own eighteenth-century brand of superstition, which is that he can wash away the sins of the world in the tears of the theater.

*C. Vann Woodward.* I believe it was friend Dick Hofsteder who said that Americans were the only people who started with perfection and then aspired to improve on it? The Enlightenment didn't start in 1787, but the first sentence of the Constitution, as you demonstrate, certainly announces this theme. Is it an earlier manifestation of a national characteristic or does it come out here first in 1787?

*Garry Wills.* It's the culmination of a great many confluent tendencies. The optimism especially of the people who took part in it, or who supported it in spirit even though they had criticisms of it in detail, including Thomas Jefferson, held that it is good to make laws often, every twenty years at least he thought, because people improve so much that it's time to get rid of the bad old laws made by our dumb grandfathers. That spirit, that we can do better than they did, that we can write a better constitution, was very strong among the people who went to Philadelphia. The people who did not go to Philadelphia, who were elected and did not go, who chose not to go, Patrick Henry, Richard Henry Lee, people like that, tended to be much more pessimistic, less optimistic about things. James Wilson, in those law lectures I've been quoting, encourages his audience, which is an audience of the public in general not simply law students, to be very active in politics because they will probably be writing a constitution someday themselves. He could believe that because he was not yet 50 years old when he said it, and had already overthrown three governments. He had personally taken part in the writing of four constitutions. He said in those lectures that "revolution" is a term of terror in other countries. In America it will be a term of benevolent change—the time when an active citizenry rewrites its laws. So there was a deep strain of optimism. Wilson brought much of this over from Scotland, took much of it from Rousseau. There is optimism in Franklin, optimism in Madison, in Jefferson. Pessimism is expressed primarily in the ratifying conventions, by people who don't want the Constitution to pass.

*John Rodgers*. In the matter of revolution you mention, sir, that Jefferson did not expect revolution during his term because he felt that 1800 had been a revolution—his election. He called it the revolution of 1800. And in fact I think you can make the case if you wish and I have tried to do so that we've had a revolution every 30 years or so since then.

*Garry Wills*. Wilson thought that elections themselves would be revolutionary acts. He said election is an act of the originating sovereignty of a society. He differed from most theorists in thinking that. But he also expected an actual rewriting of the Constitution, as did Jefferson. So they thought that there was some revolution in 1800, but they expected even more and wanted more.

*Sir Christopher Booth*. One of the features of the Enlightenment that intrigues one is the use of language in the reflection by Dr. Johnson in his dictionary of the views of John Locke in his fourth book. And one just wonders. You dwelt a bit upon the use of language in the writing of the Constitution. They referred to the use of prepositional phrases. What sort of linguistic model did they use? Did they use a dictionary to define the terms that they included in their Constitution?

*Garry Wills*. Much of their use of language was legal. And legal terminology is fixed, very stable and conservative. For instance in *Federalist* 10—that's a document that's often misread because Madison says that when people are ready to set up a faction, and a faction for him is always a conspiracy against the rights of someone else—in a domain of larger extent, people will have a harder time "discovering" their strength throughout the country. Now that is almost invariably read to mean that people cannot find out what so and so is thinking far off in another part of the country, but discovery of intent in legal terminology had a very fixed meaning and still does. *Discovery* is a normal term in law. It means reveal your position. It meant that people will be too ashamed to reveal on a broad scale that they are plotting against the rights of others. There will be an inhibition, part of the public sense of shame. So there he was working not from popular usage or Johnson's dictionary or the French encyclopedia, but from established legal usage. And a good deal of the language is simply a new use of old legal language. Wilson takes his law lectures and models them exactly on Blackstone. He says I am going to do what Blackstone did, but I am going to come out with a totally different result, because we have a totally different system. And he takes each point of language and redefines it. But he begins with legal terminology. Thus "a more perfect union" was a term that had been around in legal language for a long time. A perfect government meant one with all its powers, a sovereign government.

# "An Instructive Monitor": Experience and the Fabrication of the Federal Constitution

**JACK P. GREENE**

*Andrew W. Mellon Professor in the Humanities, The Johns Hopkins University*

From the perspective of the constitutional history of the modern era, the achievement of the fifty-five men who came together in Philadelphia during the late spring and summer of 1787 to fabricate the federal Constitution seems little short of remarkable, an achievement that may perhaps even be deserving to be called the "Miracle at Philadelphia," the title of both Catherine Drinker Bowen's evocative narrative of the Convention of twenty years ago and the excellent exhibit currently mounted down the street by the Friends of Independence National Historical Park.[1] Certainly, contemporary supporters and opponents of the Constitution were fully aware of what the Massachusetts delegate Elbridge Gerry referred to in the Convention as the "novelty and difficulty of the experiment."[2] "The novelty of the undertaking immediately strikes us," its principal architect James Madison admitted in *Federalist* #37,[3] while Patrick Henry, one of its most vociferous adversaries, denounced it as a "perilous innovation," "an entire alteration of government," a hodgepodge of "novelties" that, taken together, comprised a government that was "so new, it wants a name."[4]

---

[1] Catherine Drinker Bowen, *Miracle at Philadelphia: The Story of the Constitutional Convention, May to September 1787* (New York, 1967).

[2] Speech, 5 June 1787, in Adrienne Koch, ed., *Notes of Debates in the Federal Convention of 1787 Reported by James Madison* (Athens, Ohio, 1985), 69.

[3] Madison, *The Federalist* (ed. Jacob E. Cooke, Middletown, Conn., 1961), #37, 233. All subsequent citations to *The Federalist* are to this edition.

[4] Speech, in Jonathan Elliot, ed., *The Debates in the Several State Conventions, on the Adoption of the Federal Constitution* (4 vols., Washington, 1836), III, 55–56.

**James Madison.**

**Engraving by William S. Leney. Courtesy of the Library Company of Philafelphia.**

Yet, historians and informed lay Americans have long understood that, however extraordinary and inventive an achievement it represented at the time and still appears to be two hundred years later, the federal Constitution was far less novel than contemporaries liked to suppose and was both deeply rooted in the socioeconomic, political, and intellectual context out of which it came and far less the product of a miracle than of hard work, a penetrating application of intellect and expertise, and considerable political compromise. Especially during the century since the celebration of the centennial of the Constitution in 1887, historians have developed a relatively sophisticated comprehension of the complex forces that lay behind and informed the formation and content of that document. For the better part of fifty years after Charles A. Beard published his seminal work, *An Economic History of the Constitution*, in 1913, they focused very heavily upon the economic and sectional divisions that both shaped the struggle over the Constitution and informed the document itself.[5] More recently, historians have stressed two additional and related aspects of the battle over the Constitution: first, the broader social and political tensions underlying that battle,[6] and, second, the extent to which it was rooted in and reflective of ideological traditions that had been inherited from Britain and Europe and were subsequently modified to meet conditions in Revolutionary America.[7]

As a consequence of this emphasis, many of the complex aspects of the specific social context of the struggle over the Constitution, what the South Carolina delegate Charles Pinckney called "the situation of our people,"[8] are now beginning to be fairly well understood. Similarly, we now have a much broader appreciation of the deep learning displayed by many of the framers

---

[5] Charles A. Beard, *An Economic Interpretation of the Constitution* (New York, 1913); Merrill Jensen, *The Articles of Confederation* (Madison, 1940), and *The New Nation: A History of the United States During the Confederation, 1781–1789* (New York, 1950); Robert E. Brown, *Charles Beard and the Constitution* (Princeton, N.J., 1956); and Forrest McDonald, *We the People: The Economic Origins of the Constitution* (Chicago, 1958).

[6] Lee Benson, *Turner and Beard: American Historical Writing Reconsidered* (Glencoe, Ill., 1960); Jackson Turner Main, *The Antifederalists: Critics of the Constitution, 1781–1788* (Chapel Hill, 1961), and *Political Parties before the Constitution* (Chapel Hill, 1973); and Forrest McDonald, *E Pluribus Unum: The Formation of the American Republic, 1776–1790* (Boston, 1965).

[7] See, especially, Gordon S. Wood, *The Creation of the American Republic, 1776–1787* (Chapel Hill, 1969); Gerald Stourzh, *Alexander Hamilton and the Idea of Republican Government* (Stanford, 1970); J. G. A. Pocock, *The Machiavellian Moment: Florentine Political Thought and the Atlantic Tradition* (Princeton, N.J., 1975); Joyce Appleby, *Capitalism and a New Social Order: The Republican Vision of the 1790s* (New York, 1984); Morton White, *The Philosophy of the American Revolution* (New York, 1978); Forrest McDonald, *Novus Ordo Seclorum: The Intellectual Origins of the Constitution* (Lawrence, Kans., 1985); Jack P. Greene, *The Intellectual Heritage of the Constitutional Era: The Delegates' Library* (Philadelphia, 1986).

[8] Speech, 25 June 1787, in Koch, ed., *Notes of Debates*, 183.

along with their indebtedness to inherited traditions of thought and their extensive use of certain celebrated works, including especially those of Montesquieu, Blackstone, and Hume. But an acute awareness of social context and solid grounding in the broad intellectual heritage of Britain and Europe were not the only ingredients that informed the calculations of the men who contrived and contended over the Constitution in the late 1780s.[9] Not surprisingly among elite figures in that age of self-conscious enlightenment, they frequently appealed, as many intellectual historians have emphasized, not just to circumstances and learned authorities but also to reason. Defined by Dr. Samuel Johnson in his *Dictionary* as the deliberative power by which people deduced "one proposition from another" or proceeded "from premises to consequences" in the effort to achieve logical and coherent perceptions of situations and problems, reason was thought of as both consistent with common sense and incompatible with passion and prejudice. Thus, with Alexander Hamilton, late eighteenth-century Americans often recommended their views as conformable "to the dictates of reason and good sense."[10]

What has perhaps tended to be somewhat underemphasized and what certainly was no less important than social context, learning, and reason in shaping action and thought in the Constitutional era was what learned men of the age referred to as "experience." In the speeches in the debates both at the convention and in the state ratifying conventions and in the polemical writings of the period, perhaps no term was more ubiquitous than "experience." "No word," Douglass Adair pointed out in a brilliant article twenty years ago, "was used more often [in the Convention debates]; time after time 'experience' was appealed to as the clinching argument."[11] Invoking experience, the principals in the debate over the Constitution urged their audiences to consult or look to experience in support of their positions. Using a broad assortment of active verbs, they declared that what they called the "concurring testimony of experience," "unequivocal experience," or "indubitable experience" either did—or did not—"fully" or "emphatically" prove, overrule, sanction, corroborate, teach, evince, confirm, deny, qualify, admonish, enforce, point out, pro-

---

[9] See, in addition to the items cited in note 7, Donald S. Lutz, "The Relative Influence of European Thinkers on Late Eighteenth-Century American Political Thought," *American Political Science Review*, 78 (1984): 189–97, and David Lundberg and Henry F. May, "The Enlightened Reader in America," *American Quarterly*, 28 (1976): 262–93.

[10] Hamilton, *Federalist*, #70, 474.

[11] Douglass G. Adair, "Experience Must Be Our Only Guide: History, Democratic Theory, and the United States Constitution," in Jack P. Greene, *The Reinterpretation of the American Revolution* (New York, 1968), 399.

duce, determine, warn against, show, satisfy, illustrate, instruct, urge, guide, inform, exemplify, ascertain, attest, convince, provide models for, or present lessons about whatever point they were trying to make.[12]

Experience, they asserted, was "the best of all tests,"[13] "the parent of wisdom,"[14] "the least fallible guide of human opinions,"[15] "the guide that ought always to be followed whenever it can be found,"[16] the "best oracle of wisdom."[17] "Experience," declared John Dickinson, "must be our only guide. Reason may mislead us."[18] "Theoretic reasoning," agreed Madison, "must [always] be qualified by the lessons of practice," that is, experience.[19] All speculation had to yield, said Hamilton, "to the natural and experienced course of human affairs."[20] Warning against "curious speculations," Melancton Smith urged his fellow delegates to the New York ratifying convention "to adopt a system, whose principles have been sanctioned by experience."[21] "Experience," echoed James Duane in the same gathering, "ought to have more influence on our conduct, than all the speculation and elaborate reasonings of the ablest men."[22] Experience, said the Maryland delegate Daniel Carroll, simply "overruled all other calculations."[23] "Where its responses are unequivocal," agreed Madison, "they ought to be conclusive and sacred."[24]

This widespread and laudatory use of the concept of experience raises two important questions: First, what did the framers and their contemporaries mean when they used the term, and, second, what were some of the more important conclusions they drew from experience?

When his colleagues elected George Washington to chair the convention, he reminded them "of the novelty of the scene of business in which he was to act, lamented his want of better qualifications, and claimed the indulgence of the House towards the involuntary errors which his inexperience might occasion."[25] Four days later in placing the Virginia Plan before the Convention,

---

[12] Koch, ed., *Notes of Debates, and Federalist*, passim.
[13] Speech of George Mason, 4 June 1787, in Koch, ed., *Notes of Debates*, 64.
[14] Hamilton, *Federalist* #72, 490.
[15] Hamilton, *Federalist* #6, 32.
[16] Madison, *Federalist* #52, 355.
[17] Hamilton, *Federalist* #15, 96.
[18] Speech, 13 August 1787, in Koch, ed., *Notes of Debates*, 447.
[19] Madison, *Federalist* #43, 293.
[20] Hamilton, *Federalist* # 25, 162.
[21] Speech, in *The Debates and Proceedings of the Convention of the State of New-York* (New York, 1805), 35.
[22] Speech, ibid., 110.
[23] Speech, 22 August 1787, in Koch, ed., *Notes of Debates*, 511.
[24] Madison, *Federalist* #20, 128.
[25] Speech, 25 May 1787, in Koch, ed., *Notes of Debates*, 24.

Washington's younger colleague, Edmund Randolph expressed his "regret, that it should fall to him, rather than [to] those, who were of longer standing in life and political experience to open the great subject of their mission."[26] Washington and Randolph, respectively, used the terms "inexperience" and "experience" on these occasions to mean personal knowledge acquired by an individual during his lifetime.

If Washington and Randolph each felt a keen sense of his lack of experience in the particular roles in which he found himself, however, the collective personal experience in public life of the delegates was enormously impressive. With Benjamin Franklin the oldest at 81 and New Jersey delegate Jonathan Dayton the youngest at 27, the mean age of the delegates was 43.5 years. Notwithstanding the relative youthfulness of many members of the group, however, and the incompleteness of the data, the delegates had a combined record of public service in provincial and continental offices of well over 750 years! The mean number of years was 13.6 and the median 11. These figures do not include service in local government. Forty-nine—all but six of the fifty-five delegates—had served in one or the other and in some cases both branches of their Colonial and state legislatures, six had been governors of states, and at least seven had taken a prominent part in the state judicial systems. Almost half—49 percent—were lawyers, who routinely in their private occupations came in contact with the public world many days every year. Twenty-two had taken an active role with the army during the War for Independence, and forty-three, just over 80 percent, had served at least one year in the Continental Congress, the mean term in Congress being 4.1 and the median 4 years. Together, they had served a total of 175 years in that body.[27]

If, as John Jay remarked in *Federalist* #2, the First Continental Congress back in 1774 had been "composed of many wise and experienced men" and "if the people at large had reason to" place their confidence "in the men of that Congress, few of whom had then been fully tried or [were] generally known" outside the boundaries of their own colonies, the public had even more reason to trust the judgment of the members of the Convention. For, as Jay explained, it was "well known that some of the most distinguished members of that Congress, who have been since tried and justly approved for patriotism

---

[26] Speech, 29 May 1787, in ibid., 28.

[27] The figures on age and number of lawyers are taken from Richard D. Brown, "The Founding Fathers of 1776 and 1787: A Collective View," *William and Mary Quarterly*, 3d ser., 33 (1976): 467, 469. The other statements in this paragraph have been computed from data in *Biographical Directory of the American Congress 1774–1971* (Washington, 1971), and Allen Johnson and Dumas Malone, eds., *The Dictionary of American Biography* (10 vols., New York, 1927–36).

and abilities, and who have grown old in acquiring political information, were also members of this Convention and carried into it their accumulated knowledge and experience."[28] "The respectability of this convention," a respectability deriving out of the extensive service and experience of its members, predicted Madison correctly on the floor of the Convention, would in itself "give weight to their recommendation[s]."[29]

As Douglass Adair pointed out in the article referred to earlier, however, the Founders used the concept of experience not simply to mean individual "political wisdom gained by participation" in public life, but also in a second and much broader sense to mean "the political wisdom gained by studying past events,"[30] what Hamilton referred to in *Federalist* #6 as "the accumulated experience of the ages."[31] This is the sense in which Madison employed the word when he told the delegates that they had "the experience of other nations before them."[32] Very often in the literature surrounding the Constitution, the terms "history" and "experience" were employed interchangeably. Thus, when Madison claimed in Convention that his observations on the tendency of majorities to violate the rights of minorities were "verified by the Histories of every Country antient & modern"[33] and when Melancton Smith announced in the New York ratifying convention that he could illustrate his argument that a large number of representatives was unnecessary to retain the confidence of the public "by a variety of historical examples, both ancient and modern,"[34] they were using "history" synonymously with "experience."

Of the several histories available to the founding generation, that of Great Britain, as John Jay remarked in *Federalist* #22, was the "one with which we are in general the best acquainted," and he agreed with Madison that it presented "to mankind . . . many political lessons, both of the monitory and exemplary kind," "useful lessons" that enabled Americans, as Jay put it, to "profit by" the British "experience without paying the price which it cost them."[35] But they also referred often to the history of confederated republics, from both the ancient world, including the Achaean League, the Amphictyonic Confederacies, and the Lycean Confederacy, and the modern world, including especially the Swiss, German, and Dutch confederacies. For the supporters

---

[28] *Federalist* #2, 11–12.
[29] Speech, 12 June 1787, in Koch, ed., *Notes of Debates*, 107.
[30] Adair, "Experience Must Be Our Only Guide," 400.
[31] *Federalist* #6, 28.
[32] Speech, 26 June 1787, in Koch, ed., *Notes of Debates*, 193.
[33] Speech, 6 June 1787, ibid., 76–77.
[34] Speech, in *Debates and Proceedings of New-York*, 37.
[35] Jay, *Federalist* #5, 24; Madison, *Federalist* #56, 382.

of the Constitution and a more energetic central government, "all the examples of other confederacies . . . fully illustrated" the "same tendency of the parts to encroach upon the whole" and "prove[d] the greater tendency in such systems to anarchy than to tyranny; to a disobedience of the members than to usurpations of the federal head"[36] By contrast, opponents of the Constitution cited the same histories to make the well-known Antifederalist point that, in George Mason's words, "there never was a government, over a very extensive country, without destroying the liberties of the people: history also, supported by the opinions of the best writers," Mason added, "shews us that monarchy may suit a large territory, and despotic . . . governments ever so extensive a country: but that popular governments can only exist in small territories."[37]

If this extensive use of experience as a synonym for history helps to establish Adair's point that the Founders' "conscious and deliberate use of history and theory" played an important part in their deliberations, he certainly overstated his case when he argued that when the Founders used the word "experience," they referred, "more often than not, to the precepts of history" conceived of as the wisdom of the ages as transmitted to America from Europe.[38] Indeed, for every person who, like Dickinson, extolled "the singular & admirable mechanism of the English Constitution" and recommended the "long experience" of Britain as a guide,[39] there were many more who, with the South Carolina delegate Pierce Butler, decried the tendency to be "always following the British Constitution when the reason of it did not apply."[40] In direct answer to Dickinson, Butler's colleague John Rutledge traced many of the defects of the state constitutions "to a blind adherence to the British model,"[41] while James Wilson insisted that "the British Model . . . was inapplicable to the situation of this Country; the extent of which was so great, and the manners so republican, that nothing but a great confederated republic would do for it."[42] "When applied to our situation which was extremely different," said Elbridge Gerry in seconding Wilson, "maxims taken from the British constitution were often fallacious."[43] In Edmund Randolph's words, the Convention

[36] Speeches, 19,21 June, in Koch, ed., *Notes of Debates*, 142–43,164–65.

[37] Speech, in Jonathan Elliott, ed., *The Debates in the Several State Conventions, on the Adoption of the Federal Constitution* (4 vols., Washington, 1836), III, 60.

[38] Adair, "Experience Must be Our Only Guide," 398–400.

[39] Speech, 13 August 1787, in Koch, ed., *Notes of Debates*, 447.

[40] Speech, 13 June 1787, ibid., 113.

[41] Speech, 13 August 1787, ibid., 448–49.

[42] Speeches, 1,7 June 1787, ibid., 47,85.

[43] Speech, 31 May 1787, ibid., 41.

had absolutely "no motive to be governed by the British Governm[en]t as our prototype."[44]

But it was not just the British experience that was of marginal relevance to the United States. "We have unwisely considered ourselves as the inhabitants of an old instead of a new country," lamented Charles Pinckney in asserting that the American situation was entirely "distinct from either the people of Greece or Rome, or of any State we are acquainted with among [either] the antients" or the moderns.[45] For five weeks, complained Roger Sherman of Connecticut on 28 June, "we have gone back to ancient history for models of Government, and examined the different forms of those Republics which having been formed with the seeds of their own dissolution now no longer exist. And we have viewed Modern States all round Europe, but find none of the Constitutions [and little of their experience] suitable to our Circumstances."[46] There was little point, Edmund Randolph told the Virginia ratifying Convention, in wasting time "with . . . historical references, which have no kind of analogy to the points under our consideration."[47]

What appears to have been far more relevant to most delegates to the Convention and probably also to most supporters of the Constitution in the state ratifying conventions was what Dickinson had dismissed as "the short experience of 11 years" that Americans had had in trying to govern themselves.[48] In their fear of a distant central power and their advocacy of local autonomy, Antifederalists showed a distinct preference for emphasizing the experience of the pre-Revolutionary years when the colonies were faced by an aggressive centralizing power in Britain.[49] By contrast, Federalists were far more impressed by the American experience with republican government in the years after 1776.

As the delegates acknowledged over and over again in Convention debates, their experience with republican government had contributed to help make the framers of the Constitution acutely aware of the political limits within which they worked. Perhaps even more than their predecessors during the

---

[44] Speech, 1 June 1787, ibid., 46.
[45] Speech, 25 June 1787, ibid., 184–85.
[46] Speech, 28 June 1787, ibid., 209.
[47] Speech, in Elliott, *Debates*, III, 94.
[48] Speech, 13 August 1787, in Koch, ed., *Notes of Debates*, 447.
[49] See on this point the excellent article by Frederick R. Black, "The American Revolution as 'Yardstick' in the Debates on the Constitution, 1787–1788," *Proceedings of the American Philosophical Society*, 117 (1973): 162–85.

Colonial period, they understood the force of that hallowed early modern political maxim that "All government . . . depend[ed] . . . in a great degree on opinion."[50] "No government," said James Wilson, "could subsist without the confidence of the people"[51] "If the Gov[ernmen]t is to be lasting," declared George Mason, it had to "be founded in the confidence & affections of the people, and must be so constructed to obtain these."[52]

More specifically, experience had taught them that no government could obtain the confidence of the American public that was not "organized in the republican form,"[53] that did not guarantee the sanctity of the existing states, that was too expensive, or that went beyond the minimal functions of securing respect abroad and maintaining "happiness & security" at home.[54] "The industrious habits of the people of the present day, absorbed in the [private] pursuit of gain, and devoted to the improvements of agriculture and commerce," Alexander Hamilton noted, were "incompatible" with a large Public realm or an expensive government.[55] People could expect no more from government, averred Charles Pinckney, than to be "capable of extending to its citizens all the blessing of civil & religious liberty—capable of making them happy at home" in the private realm.[56]

But their "own experience" with independent republican government beginning in 1776 had not only underlined for American political leaders the popular limits of political action; it had also revealed a wide variety of perplexing problems.[57] "Experience had evinced" a want of energy in the central government, an absence of "an effectual control in the whole over its parts," and "a constant tendency in the States to encroach on the federal authority; to violate national Treaties; [and] to infringe the rights & interests of each other."[58] Within the states, moreover, "experience had"[59] where "the mischievous influence of demagogues" and a palpable lack of regard for minority rights and interests produced a "multiplicity of laws" characterized by their

[50] Speech of Melancton Smith, *Debates and Proceedings of New-York*, 36.
[51] Speech, 31 May 1787, in Koch, ed., *Notes of Debate*, 41.
[52] Speech, 29 August 1787, in Koch, ed., *Notes of Debate*, 549.
[53] Madison's Speech, 12 June 1787, in Koch, ed., *Notes of Debate*, 111.
[54] Speech, 25 June 1787, in Koch, ed., *Notes of Debate*, 185.
[55] Hamilton, *Federalist* #8, 47.
[56] Speech, 25 June 1787, in Koch, ed., *Notes of Debate*, 185.
[57] Speech of Wilson, 20 June 1787, in Koch, ed., *Notes of Debate*, 162.
[58] Speeches of Madison, 7 June 1787, and Wilson, 8 June 1987, in Koch, ed., *Notes of Debate*, 88, 91.
[59] Speech of Madison, 17 July 1787, in Koch, ed., *Notes of Debate*, 312.

"mutability," "injustice," and "impotence."[60] To "check the precipitation, changeableness, and excesses" of the state legislatures,[61] to "protect the people ag[ain]st those speculating Legislatures which" at that very moment were "plundering them throughout the United) States,"[62] experience told them, required a two-house legislature and a strong executive.

The hope of remedying these and many other "evils" they had "experienced" after 1776 inspired the framers to attempt a bold new experiment in framing an extended republic of a kind never before attempted, and they cautiously hoped that what they had contrived might be less flawed than they suspected. If, however, in the process of making their great contribution to the "science of politics,"[63] the Founders had "paid a decent regard to the opinions of former times and other nations," they also, as Madison said in *Federalist* #14, had never "suffered a blind veneration for antiquity, for custom, or for names, to overrule the suggestions of their own good sense, the knowledge of their own situation, and the lessons of their own experience."[64] Their own collective experience with republican government, Madison thus suggested almost certainly correctly, was the most important of the several empirical foundations of the Constitution.

---

[60] Speeches of Madison, 19 June 1787, and Randolph, 13 August 1787, in Koch, ed., *Notes of Debate*, 145, 443.

[61] Speech of Gouverneur Morris, 2 July 1787, in Koch, ed., *Notes of Debate*, 233.

[62] Speech of John Francis Mercer, 14 August 1787, in Koch, ed., *Notes of Debate*, 451.

[63] Hamilton, *Federalist* #9, 51.

[64] Madison, *Federalist* #14, 88.

# *Franklin, Washington, and a New Nation*

**John Shy**

*The University of Michigan*

Nothing is more important, or more elusive, than the idea of fundamental law.[1] However tiresome obligatory anniversary celebrations may be, the bicentennial chance to think again about the fundamental law of the United States is welcome, especially if it causes us to look at the subject more carefully than we usually do. Our natural tendency with a subject so centrally important is to treat what we know as if it were something like a body of fact, reserving our critical and creative energies for newer, fresher, more immediately urgent subjects. The Constitution sits in our mind like a great, familiar building; we know it well, we pass through it frequently, we even work in it, but we scarcely see it and rarely think of it. We are less sensitive to some of its features than an outsider might be, who would find it exotic, impressive, and puzzling. So we can take this imposed chance to stop and look more closely at the edifice, and at how it was built, with the unschooled, sensible eyes of the outsider who sees things so obvious that we miss them.[2]

Among the most obvious yet puzzling of these things is the role played in shaping our fundamental law by those two senior revolutionaries, the first Americans to achieve international fame—Benjamin Franklin and George Washington.

Begin the inquiry with two apparently unrelated, dissimilar statements: First, that these two great leaders of the American Revolution, Franklin and

---

[1] Ronald Dworkin, *Law's Empire* (Cambridge, Mass.: Harvard University Press, 1986), is a recent, stimulating attempt to deal with the interpretation and application of law. He points out, on p. 355, that if the Supreme Court under John Marshall had not claimed the power to interpret it, "The Constitution would then have played a very different and much weaker role in American politics."

[2] To Professor Arthur S. Link I owe the basic question asked in this essay, and to Dr. Jonathan Marwil I owe a friendly, critical reading of the first version of the answer.

Washington, gave the Constitution their blessing and lent it their enormous prestige, but in 1786–87 they were surprisingly indifferent to its details, to the crucially important attempt to define the new structure of the American republic; and second, that if George B. McClellan had won the Presidential election of 1864, chances are none of us would be celebrating the Constitution today, or if we were, we would be talking about 1787 in a very different way. What follows is an exploration of the meaning of these statements, an attempt to connect them, and from this connection an effort to develop a better, more truly historical way of seeing how our fundamental law took shape in 1787.

General McClellan losing the election of 1864, after running on a platform of negotiating an end to the war with the Confederate States, while (in the process of losing the election) winning 45 percent of the popular vote, suggests that our view of the Constitution is profoundly anachronistic. We see it in terms of its enduring success, when of course its success remained problematical, not only in 1787 but for about a century thereafter. A President McClellan would almost certainly, in one way or another, have demonstrated that the Philadelphia Convention was a failure, accurately foreshadowed by a history since 1789 of almost decennial constitutional crises.[3] The Canadians did not wait for the 1864 election to prove the point; they already understood it very well, and in 1864—frightened by what they saw to the southward—were busy fashioning a constitution of their own (to be blessed by Her Majesty's Government in 1867) that was explicitly designed to avoid the serious mistakes made by the Americans at Philadelphia.[4]

In short, we have tended to take Constitutional success for granted, and instead to dwell on the elaborate yet delphic phrases that describe the federal structure, and on the "intent" (revealed and concealed by the surviving evidence) behind those phrases. And of course we do this because that structure and those defining phrases have had enormous and continuing consequences,

---

[3] *Guide to U.S. Elections*, published by Congressional Quarterly (Washington, 1975), conveniently provides both the key sections of the Democratic platform (pp. 38–39) and the popular vote by States (p. 272). Of course eleven States, none of whom would have voted for Lincoln, did not take part in the election.

[4] W. L. Morton, *The Critical Years: The Union of British North America, 1857–1873* (Toronto: McClelland and Stewart, 1964), 87–97, 132–39, 148–65, 203–08; Donald Creighton, *John A. Macdonald: The Young Politician* (Toronto: Macmillan of Canada, 1952), 318–21, 365, 371–81, 389–90, 403. The chief "mistake" at Philadelphia was, in the Canadian view, to have left the States too strong, the central government too weak. The irony seems to be that, whatever the Canadian and British intentions of the 1860s, the Canadian Constitution of the late 1980s, in its actual operation, resembles less the U.S. constitution than it does the Articles of Confederation. At this writing, the fate of Prime Minister Brian Mulroney's initiative (the so-called "Meech Lake Accord") to secure Quebec's assent to the 1982 Constitution is uncertain, but it seems likely that all the provinces of Canada will claim for themselves, at the expense of federal power, whatever concessions are made to Quebec, including the right to veto amendment of the Constitution. In this respect, the opposition to the Meech Lake Accord of Pierre Trudeau—a French Canadian passionately committed to a unified Canada under its own constitution—is instructive.

causing complex problems for the nation, while giving employment to generations of jurists, lawyers, legal scholars, and even ordinary historians. But without the success of the federal Constitution, which can be measured only by what came after 1787, this whole celebratory effort would be a little silly, although not even one small fact about that year would have been changed. If the Constitution had failed in 1799, or 1815, or 1820, or 1832, or 1850, or 1856, as it apparently did in 1860, or might well have done in 1864, or in 1876, then we would have a different scholarly agenda for its study, as well as far less power to attract the resources that are sponsoring the current celebration.

Historians have never tried hard enough to do for the federal Constitution what they excel in doing for other subjects: restoring to the constitutional movement of the 1780s its historical integrity, its actual sense of priorities, which did not make the precise structural details of American government nearly as important as we—following in the footsteps of an aging James Madison—have subsequently made them appear to be.[5]

Which brings us back to the first statement, that Franklin and Washington showed relatively little interest in these structural details, in things like bicameral legislatures, strict separation of powers, the nature of representation, the possibilities of judicial review, or the place of state governments in a federal system. Franklin, in his most important intervention in the Philadelphia debates, begged his colleagues to be less rigid and dogmatic in designing the new central government, and to come more quickly to some effective agreement.[6] Neither man seemed especially concerned by what ever since has

---

[5]The work of William W. Crosskey, *Politics and the Constitution in the History of the United States*, 2 vols. (Chicago: University of Chicago Press, 1953), is an extreme case, but not untypical. His work virtually reduces the word "national" to the commerce clause of the Constitution, and is an unremitting assault on judicial review in terms of original intent. A posthumous Volume III, completed by William Jeffrey, Jr. (1980), subtitled *The Political Background of the Federal Convention*, is of special interest to this essay. Among other valuable works that treat the 1780s as a field on which to re-fight later battles of American history are Merrill Jensen, *The New Nation* (New York: Alfred A. Knopf, 1950), and William P. Murphy, *The Triumph of Nationalism* (Chicago: Quadrangle Books, 1967).

[6]Franklin's speech of 28 June in favor of opening each meeting with prayer—a suggestion that to some delegates must have seemed bizarre coming from Franklin—has revealing passages: "establishing our national felicity" was the task of the Convention, and the chief danger was that "we shall succeed in this political building no better than the Builders of Babel: We shall be divided by our little partial local interests; our projects will be confounded, and we ourselves shall become a reproach and bye word down to future ages." *The Records of the Federal Convention of 1787*, edited by Max Farrand, revised edition, 4 vols. (New Haven, Conn.: Yale University Press, 1937), 1: 451–52. It was on the final day of the Convention, 17 September, that James Wilson read aloud the speech written by Franklin, who said that he could not approve several parts of the proposed Constitution, but that he would sign it and support it "because I think a general Government necessary for us . . . and I think it will astonish our enemies, who are waiting with confidence to hear . . . that our States are on the point of separation, only to meet hereafter for the purpose of cutting one another's throats. Thus I consent, Sir, to this Constitution because I expect no better. . . . " Ibid., 2: 642–43.

been our Constitutional preoccupation. Why? That question of course has a standard answer.

The standard answer is that Franklin was old, indeed dying, tired of the hustle-bustle of politics. Indeed, Franklin was otherwise engaged during the mid-1780s, in the salons of Paris, reluctant to give up in the last years of a long life his God-like status in France and come home to the dusty, democratic streets of Philadelphia. But return he did, to help draft and support the new Constitution, and then to fade away, to immortality. It is known that Franklin preferred representation by population, and a unicameral legislature like that in Pennsylvania, but if he had more specific ideas about the design of the new government, or even about the nature of the American society that this government would try to restrain and protect, he buried them in his *Autobiography* or took them to his grave. He intervened in the Convention debate on proportional representation, but chiefly to argue the case for compromise by exposing the problems in any system of representation.[7]

The standard answer for Washington is that he was no political scientist, a great soldier and patriot to be sure, but not equipped intellectually or educationally to play in the same fast league with the constitutional likes of Hamilton, Madison, Adams, or Jay.[8] Others would have to design the monarchical presidency that he was destined to occupy. The ideas of Washington about government seem few and simple; above all, he hated factionalism and disorder, as befits a military commander, and could tolerate popular participation in government only within constitutionally prescribed limits.[9]

Both Washington and Franklin were in fact deeply concerned by the American political situation in 1786–87—Washington as anxious as anyone in the country, and Franklin by no means apathetic or confident about those

[7] Ibid., 1: 197–200. Anyone who reads Franklin's correspondence for these last years of his life will be impressed by his energy, and disinclined to conclude that his mental powers were fading. He showed more interest in defending the controversial Pennsylvania constitution of 1776, and even applying its principles to national government, than in engaging in debates on the specific proposals put before the Philadelphia Convention.

[8] Hamilton, in the midst of a dispute with Washington in 1781, described him as slowwitted and stubborn. *The Papers of Alexander Hamilton*, ed. Harold C. Syrett et al., 26 vols. (New York: Columbia University Press, 1961–79), 2: 567.

[9] When asked in 1786 for his opinion of a "Patriotic Society" formed in the Virginia tidewater to consider "the state of public affairs," Washington replied: "Generally speaking, I have seen as much evil as good result from such Societies . . . ; they are a kind of imperium in imperio, and as often clog as facilitate public measures. . . . To me it appears much wiser and more politic, to choose able and honest representatives, and leave them in all national questions to determine from the evidence of reason, and the facts . . . " To Bushrod Washington, 30 Sept. 1786, *The Writings of George Washington*, ed. John C. Fitzpatrick, 39 vols. (Washington: U.S. Government Printing Office, 1931–44), 29: 22.

matters that so troubled Washington. Franklin and Washington were, in this respect, fairly representative of most of their fellow Americans. What worried them, and almost everyone else, was less the prospect of constitutional breakdown under the Articles of Confederation than the imminent breakup of the United States.

These are not the same set of fears described in different words. Franklin, foreshadowing the Progressive school of modern historians, seemed ready to believe that the United States might even continue under the Articles of Confederation if divisive forces, between states and regions, could only be reduced. Washington, keeping rather different company in his correspondence, was persuaded that a more radical revision of existing central government was required. But both men shared a fixation on a single object: Not on democratic stability, or on republican virtue, or on freedom for capitalist enterprise, but on the nation itself, on the maintenance of national integrity. Virtually all else was seen by them, and by the great majority of their countrymen, as subordinate to the overriding national goal.

What excited and alarmed Franklin and Washington was the manifest threat to their own belief in the value and the viability of the American nation. Of course that nation embodied workable democracy, the virtues of republican government, and freedom for the kind of enterprise that had long filled the busy lives of both men. But the point, missed so easily, is that none of these aspects of polity were considered or even imagined on a reduced geographical scale, as being viable in a republic of Virginia, or Pennsylvania, or New England. Never did either man ever suggest that freedom, equality, and goodness might be better achieved and maintained by smaller geographical units, independent of one another as they had become independent of Great Britain.[10]

Such a thought, had it ever been entertained, would have been not only plausible, but firmly grounded in classical republican theory, in which small

[10] Admittedly this point, like much of this essay, has to be argued by inference from silence as well as from context. Paul C. Nagel, *One Nation Indivisible: The Union in American Thought, 1776–1861* (New York: Oxford University Press, 1964), is the standard work on its subject. Although Nagel's research is valuable, I disagree completely with his interpretation of evidence, and with his general argument that the intense American nationalism of the mid-nineteenth century emerged from a tentative, purely instrumental sense of national unity in the Revolutionary period—"a means rather than an end" (p. 16). The work suffers from an unduly literal reading of texts, and perhaps from an assumption that the "story" must "progress" from "weak" to "strong." To cite a single example: Washington's statement in late 1785, "If we are afraid to trust one another . . . there is an end of the Union," is treated as evidence of weak or qualified attachment to national integrity (p. 15); I read it in the opposite sense. The original letter, and other letters written at the same time, may be found in *Writings of Washington*, 28: 328 and adjacent pages.

countries were deemed suitable, but big ones—like Poland and the United States—dangerously unstable.[11] And yet neither man, nor Americans in general as far as we can tell, would argue for the de-federalization of the Revolutionary Republic as a possible solution to the current crisis, even though that crisis seemed to threaten the predictable degeneration of democracy and independence into anarchy or dictatorship.

Far less important than the specific structure of American government was the maintenance of the American nation, in its fullest territorial extent, the territorial nation as it had emerged from a long war for independence. This view, defying both classical theory and dire prophecy, was held by Franklin, Washington, and their fellow Americans of the 1780s as an article of religious faith.[12] That faith, I submit, more than any other factor, accounts for the constitutional movement. Even better, it explains the grudging acquiescence of Americans in what most of them regarded as the dubious piece of work done by the Philadelphia Convention. They doubted, and many would continue to doubt, but the greater evil of national breakup still loomed, and they finally gave in, during the ratification process, and later.[13]

It seems implausible that the main point of this essay, on the overwhelming importance to the establishment of American fundamental law in the 1780s of national consciousness and commitment, could be both new and true. If new, surely it could not be true, for better historians long ago would have established a point of such importance. But the great difficulty in seeing the point lies chiefly in the subsequent history of the Constitution itself, especially in the endless, violent argument over the exact nature of American federalism. Very early in that argument, the words "federal," "anti-federal," and "national" became emotionally charged—weapons in the fights that broke out in the 1790s over power, interest, and ideology. And those fights have gone on, and on. During the twentieth century, followers of Charles Beard have fought a legion of critics, in effect rehearsing the old battles between Hamiltonians and Jeffersonians.

"National," with its correlative "ist" and "ism," by being polemicized has lost much of its breadth and flexibility as a way of thinking about the

---

[11] The classic exposure and refutation of the idea that republicanism can flourish only in small territories is by James Madison. *The Federalist*, No. 10.

[12] The postwar importance of the specific—and peculiar—territorial outcome of the Revolutionary War is sensitively explored by Peter S. Onuf, *The Origins of the Federal Republic: Jurisdictional Controversies in the United States, 1775–1787* (Philadelphia: University of Pennsylvania Press, 1983).

[13] The point emphatically made by Charles A. Beard, *An Economic Interpretation of the Constitution of the United States* (New York: Macmillan, 1913; 1935 ed.), pp. 251–52 and elsewhere, stands unrefuted.

formative period of the United States. The word, except in any but the most general usage, has been equated with a specific form of polity: a strong central government whose power logically diminishes the power of the states. The bitterness of the American debate over state sovereignty, and over state's rights versus "federal" encroachment, has made it almost impossible not to confound "national" consciousness with a specific idea of governmental structure.

The Beardians have long argued their case in terms of something like a "nationalist" conspiracy in the 1780s to give more power to Congress at the expense of the states, a conspiracy resisted by those who defended state interests, who disliked all governmental power, or who cherished popular democracy. The critics of Beardianism, by insisting that a stronger central government in the 1780s was intended to save democracy, not subvert it, have further obscured the independent role of national sentiment as a distinct value. Even the most sophisticated, open-minded students of the period, like Gordon Wood, become engrossed in the complexities of the debate over structure, and adopt the language of the polemicists, with the result that the vital point about nationalism simply vanishes. No one argued it, so presumably it did not exist.[14]

Historians may have slighted the importance of American nationalism in the constitutional movement because it is too obvious, too simple, and slips too easily into panegyric more suitable for political speeches than serious scholarship. They may also have slighted the nationalism of the 1780s because its more robust, assertive, spread-eagle manifestation a generation or two later, during the Age of Andrew Jackson, has misled some of them into seeing this later period as formative. But looked at squarely and carefully, as the lives of Franklin and Washington enable us to do, eighteenth-century American national consciousness yields something more interesting than patriotic incantation.

Behind this early nationalism lay of course the school of Realpolitik, exemplified by Alexander Hamilton, its most articulate—and most extreme—spokesman, a school to which Franklin and Washington most certainly belonged.[15] Viewed realistically, the former colonies could surely survive if they remained united. Separated into two or more independent republics, they would be prey to their natural conflicts of interest, which in turn would make

---

[14] Gordon S. Wood, *Creation of the American Republic, 1776–1787* (Chapel Hill, N.C.: University of North Carolina Press, 1969). Wood has edited a useful compendium of the differing views of modern historians in The Confederation and the Constitution (Boston: Little, Brown, 1973).

[15] The work of Gerald Stourzh is especially valuable in this respect: *Benjamin Franklin and American Foreign Policy* (Chicago: University of Chicago Press, 1954), and *Alexander Hamilton and the Idea of Republican Government* (Stanford: Stanford University Press, 1970).

them easy targets for intervention by Britain, France, or Spain; in effect, a transatlantic Poland.

But there was much more to early American nationalism than the utilitarian arguments of international power politics. It is not beyond question that a coalition or league of independent American republics would have been doomed to the internecine squabbles and dreary round of foreign intervention that make modern Balkan or Latin American history such unhappy reading. The newly independent states remained, after all, more than three thousand miles from a disunited Europe. Given the unsolvable problem of slavery south of the Potomac, the angular quality of New England culture, and the rampant settlement of the Trans-Appalachian valleys, a reasonable case can also be made in favor of separation and autonomous cooperation, as opposed to a stronger American central government. The logic of *Realpolitik* in 1787 cut in more than one direction.

Recognition that the United States was attempting to unify three or four different, antagonistic societies—East and West, North and South—was widespread in the 1780s. Washington's expressed distaste, upon his arrival at Boston in 1775, for the mores of the average New Englander is well known.[16] That John Adams detested his colleague, Benjamin Franklin, is equally well known, and may fairly be described as a clash of cultures—obsessive Yankeedom confronting permissive Pennsylvania.[17] There is simply too much contrary evidence, like these two anecdotes, to argue seriously that the United States in 1787 was some kind of "natural" national unit whose logic imposed itself, more or less unconsciously, on the Founding Fathers. It would be more nearly correct to say that the United States in 1787 was an improbable political construct, supported the more tenaciously the more its logical and actual bases became visibly tenuous.

* * *

So whence cometh this American national religion of the 1780s? Again, the lives of Washington and Franklin point to an answer. The answer is not that American national consciousness had been welling up, silently but

[16] Douglas S. Freeman, *George Washington*, 6 vols. (New York: Charles Scribner's Sons,1948–54), 3: 526.
[17] William B. Evans, "John Adams' Opinion of Benjamin Franklin," *Pennsylvania Magazine of History and Biography* 92 (1968): 220–38.

inexorably, out of the depths of Colonial existence. Of course, given the desire to do so, it may be possible to make a case for an increasing sense of distinct identity among Colonial Americans, whether as a general phenomenon or as seen in the lives of these two leaders. If we assume that American national consciousness must have been operative and increasing before the 1770s, we may indeed find some evidence in the late Colonial decades to support our assumption.

Franklin's pamphlet, *Observations Concerning the Increase of Mankind,* written in 1751 but not published until 1755, can be cited to demonstrate Franklin's early belief in the future greatness of America. His leading role during the same period in the Albany conference, called by the British Board of Trade in 1754 to coordinate Colonial Indian policy on the eve of a new war with France, may also be seen as a concrete expression of early American national identity; his plan for a permanent union of the colonies seems to foreshadow the Constitution, although it was rejected or ignored by all the Colonial governments, and it never came before the Board of Trade.[18]

Similarly, Washington's mythic encounter in 1755 with the British General Edward Braddock, who supposedly rejected the shrewd young colonel's advice to use *American* tactics in marching through the wilderness, and who thereby led his army into ambush and annihilation by Indians and their French allies, can be invoked to illustrate the emergent separate, self-conscious identity of Colonial "Americans" like Franklin and Washington.[19] A modern scholar has even done a "content analysis" of the late Colonial press to demonstrate that the rising frequency of words like "American" indicate a growing national consciousness in the Colonial population.[20] But all this is to read the history of Revolutionary America backwards, from the emergence of the United States back to the first signs of its origins in the Colonial period; instead, we ought to consider *all* the evidence of that earlier period, reading those apparent "signs" of emergent American nationalism, not in the light of the future, but in their own temporal context.

Both in his 1751 pamphlet on population growth and in his performance at Albany in 1754, the dominant idea in Franklin's mind was the concept of "empire." Britain, in its fullest imperial extent, was his only rationale for

[18] *The Papers of Benjamin Franklin,* eds. Leonard W. Labaree, William B. Willcox et al., in progress (New Haven, Conn.: Yale University Press, 1959–), 4: 225–34, 5: 275–80, 335–38, 344–53, 357–92.

[19] Freeman, *Washington,* 2: 1–102. A brief, critical account of the evidence is Bernhard Knollenberg, *George Washington: The Virginia Period, 1732–1775* (Durham, N.C.: Duke University Press, 1964), 36–43, 152–55.

[20] Richard L. Merritt, *Symbols of American Community, 1735–1775* (New Haven, Conn.: Yale University Press, 1966).

unifying and strengthening the links between parts of the empire. His exclusive concern with the British Empire led him, in the first edition of the *Observations*, to deplore the immigration of Germans to Pennsylvania—"Palatine boors" he called them—as well as the importation of Africans, less because he disliked slavery than because they would "darken" the predominantly English Colonial population.[21] The American colonies by 1750 were rapidly losing their homogeneously British ethnic quality and becoming—none more so than Pennsylvania—the melting-pot mixture of races and ethnic groups that America has been ever since.[22] It was this aspect of population growth that troubled Franklin in the 1750s; that is, he personally disliked the very aspect of a changing society that would distinguish American national identity from its British roots. Similarly, his proposal at Albany for a Colonial union was aimed solely at making the empire a more effective military organization in the face of the French and Indian threat. Late in life, he remembered the Albany conference as a great missed opportunity; by unifying the colonies, the subsequent need to tax them to pay for their own defense could have been avoided.[23] In no sense, then, was his Albany proposal an expression of American differentness or separateness.

"Pensilvania is my Darling," he wrote in 1755 to his British friend and colleague Richard Jackson, and if Franklin had a focus for loyalty and commitment aside from the British Empire it was not "America" but his own province, Pennsylvania. A decade later those twin loyalties were most clearly seen when Franklin, as the leader and lobbyist in London for the dominant faction in the provincial Assembly, campaigned to wrest control of Pennsylvania from the Penn family proprietors by having Britain take over its government, making Pennsylvania a royal colony.[24] Even in 1764, when the first British steps toward imperial civil war were being taken, Franklin showed nothing that can be discerned as incipient American nationalism.

The case of the much younger Washington is equally clear. As an ambitious commander of Virginia troops in the 1750s, he wanted above all to be

[21] Carl Van Doren, *Benjamin Franklin* (New York: Viking Press, 1938), 216–18. These passages, later omitted, are in *Papers of Franklin* 4:234.

[22] James Henretta, *The Evolution of American Society, 1700–1815* (Lexington, Mass.: D. C. Heath, 1973), is an especially good general account of this process.

[23] *The Autobiography of Benjamin Franklin*, ed. Max Farrand (Berkeley and Los Angeles: University of California Press, 1949), 160.

[24] To Richard Jackson, 7 October 1755, *Papers of Franklin*, 6: 217. Van Doren, 306–17, briefly describes the complex politics of Pennsylvania, which are fully explored in James H. Hutson, *Pennsylvania Politics, 1746–1770* (Princeton, N.J.: Princeton University Press, 1972); and William S. Hanna, *Benjamin Franklin and Pennsylvania Politics* (Stanford, CA: Stanford University Press, 1964).

granted a royal military commission, to escape his merely "American" military status by being made a real officer of the crown.[25] Fulsome expressions of loyalty to the Empire and its sovereign—"the best of Kings," whether old George II or his grandson George III—litter Washington's early writings. And, like Franklin, Washington was also loyal not to some abstract "America," but to his own province, Virginia.

In fact, Washington gained a certain notoriety among senior British officers in 1758, when he went beyond all bounds of discretion in trying to divert the route for attack on Fort Duquesne (modern Pittsburgh) away from Pennsylvania and back to its former line of 1755, through Virginia and Maryland. The able British general, John Forbes, and his military staff saw Washington, not without reason, as a parochial Virginian, obsessed with saving the profits from large military expenditures for the port town of Alexandria on the Potomac, and with getting the benefits of an improved wagon road westward for Virginia land speculators, while denying them to rivals in Pennsylvania. Exasperated, Forbes wrote that

> Colonel Washington and my friend Colonel [William] Byrd [III] . . . were the only people I had met with who had shewed their weakness in their attachment to the Province they belong to, by declaring so publickly in favor of one road without their knowing any thing of the other, having never heard from any Pennsylvania person one word about the road.[26]

As if to underscore the point, Franklin wrote less than a year later to the British Treasury Board that Pennsylvania at great effort and expense had been covering the frontiers of Maryland, Delaware, New Jersey, New York, and Virginia, but "has not receiv'd, nor is likely to receive from any of those Provinces the least Contribution or Compensation in Consideration of the said Services and Expences."[27]

On the eve of the troubles that would lead to revolution, this mixture of imperial pride and provincial loyalty, so evident in the careers of Franklin and Washington, was typical of Colonial Americans. Historians who have depicted them as bursting with proto-national ambitions, as contemptuous of imperial laws like the Navigation Acts as they were of the supercilious manners of royal officials, are simply repeating national mythology. The reputation of

---

[25] Knollenberg, *Washington*, 44–50, 160–63, brings the evidence together on this matter.

[26] Forbes to Colonel Henry Bouquet, Raystown [PA], 23 Sept. 1758, *The Papers of Henry Bouquet*, edited by S. K. Stevens et al. (Harrisburg, 1951), 2: 536–37.

[27] April 1759, *Papers of Franklin*, 8: 334.

Colonial Americans as defiant smugglers of goods banned or heavily taxed by Acts of Parliament—a reputation proudly and routinely paraded in American history textbooks—actually pales in comparison with the truly big-time smuggling going on in and around the British Isles during the same period. In fact, American pride in being part of a victorious empire was tinged only by routine grievances—the usual stuff of any political system—and by extravagant hopes in 1763 for the imperial future.

American nationalism was not a cause of the American Revolution. As purely provincial as their contemporaries, Franklin and Washington had fought in the 1750s to defend the interests of Pennsylvania and Virginia, respectively, against the competing demands of the other province. What they had had in common was membership in the British Empire, and their shared belief—demonstrated in a variety of particular, personal ways—in the greatness of that Empire. Their commitment to a purely American national empire came suddenly, and it came directly out of their own traumatic decision and heroic effort to break away from the old Empire.

Their transition from imperial and provincial loyalties to national consciousness was not gradual but quite rapid, as it was for many Americans. Their conversion came less directly out of a decade of lawyerly disputes over constitutional rights and powers within the British Empire than narrative histories of the American Revolution usually suggest. No doubt a rising sense of frustration after 1763, even some alienation from a polity that they, so recently, had admired so much, prepared the way for conversion. But conversion itself came late and quickly, a little sooner perhaps than for most of their countrymen, and it can almost be pinpointed in time.

For Franklin, it began with the notorious interview before the British Privy Council and its guests in January 1774, when he was publicly humiliated, called a thief (as well as a "wily American") by the Solicitor General, and subsequently dismissed as Postmaster for North America. It ended a year later in the House of Lords, where the Earl of Sandwich, speaking for the government, vehemently opposed Lord Chatham's plan for reconciliation with the colonies. Sandwich then turned directly to Franklin, who was in the gallery, and expressed his contempt for the peace plan, which he said could not have been drafted by any British peer, but must have been the work of an American, like Franklin—"one of the bitterest and most mischievous Enemies this Country had ever known."[28]

[28] Quotations are from ibid., 21: 50, 581.

Writing his long account of the year just past during the voyage home to Philadelphia in March 1775, Franklin recalled that this performance and the speeches from the other Lords that followed

> made their Claim of Sovereignty over three Millions of virtuous sensible People in America, seem the greatest of Absurdities, since they appear'd to have scarce Discretion enough to govern a Herd of Swine.

Just before he left London, he again visited the House of Lords, where he was disgusted

> by many base Reflections on American Courage, Religion, Understanding &c., in which we were treated with the utmost Contempt, as the lowest of Mankind, and almost of a different Species from the English of Britain. . . .

Although others would flaunt their revolutionary radicalism during the months and years that followed, none was more intransigent, none a more implacable American, than Franklin.[29]

While Franklin underwent conversion in London, Washington experienced something comparable on the lower Potomac. The man who had once begged for a British commission, and who would later deplore extraconstitutional societies as politically dangerous, in 1774 felt emotions as powerful as those that had converted Franklin. Washington not only lost his temper—not a rare event in any case—but can be clearly seen through the surviving evidence as having been seized by a cold rage that left him a different man.

It came upon him, as such things sometimes do, in what started as rational discussion with an old friend, a neighbor, Bryan Fairfax, with whom Washington liked to hunt foxes. In June, 1774, Washington had expressed his views in a lightly punctuated letter to Bryan's brother in England, George William Fairfax:

> . . . the [British] Ministry may rely on it that Americans will never be tax'd without their consent that the cause of Boston the despotick Measures in respect to it I mean now is and ever will be considerd as the cause of America (not that we approve their conduct in destroying the Tea) and that we shall not suffer ourselves to be sacrificed by piece meals though god only knows what is to become of us, threatened as we are with so many hovering evils as hang over us at present.[30]

---

[29] His "Journal of Negotiations in London," written (like his famous *Autobiography*) as a letter to his son William, is ibid., pp. 540–99. The quotations are from pp. 583 and 598.

[30] 10 June 1774, *Writings of Washington*, 3: 224. This paragraph appears in a letter mainly about other, more mundane matters.

As far as we know, this was his first written comment on the Boston Tea Party, six months earlier. But the real explosion came a few weeks later, when neighbor Bryan suggested that a petition to Parliament, a little patience and good will, might be the best way to resolve the present crisis, triggered by the Tea Party and escalated by the Coercive Acts.

In three letters to Bryan Fairfax, from early July to late August, Washington wrote an essay on revolutionary politics. It is the passion as much as the overt message of this essay that comes through to us:

> Does it not appear, as clear as the sun in its meridian brightness, that there is a regular, systematic plan . . . ? . . . Is not the attack upon the liberty and property of the people of Boston, before restitution of the loss to the India Company was demanded, a plain and self-evident truth of what they are aiming at? Do not the subsequent bills (now I dare say acts) . . . convince us that the administration is determined to stick at nothing to carry its point? Ought we not, then, to put our virtue and fortitude to the severest test?[31]

In the second and third letters, as Fairfax argued his case for moderation and conciliation, Washington's words change but not the ideas or the feeling:

> . . . I am convinced, as much as I am of my existence, that there is no relief but in their distress; and I think, at least I hope, that there is public virtue enough left among us to deny ourselves every thing but the bare necessaries of life to acomplish [*sic*] this end. This we have a right to do, and no power upon earth can compel us to do otherwise, . . . [32]

Near the end of this remarkable exchange, just before his departure as a delegate to the congress called to meet in Philadelphia, he refers obliquely to blood being spilled, and then raises the spectre well known to every Virginian,

> . . . the crisis is arrived when we must assert our rights, or submit to every imposition, that can be heaped upon us, till custom and use shall make us as tame and abject slaves, as the blacks we rule over with such arbitrary sway.[33]

Washington, like Franklin, saw himself as a moderate, sensible man, not disposed to impulsive words or acts; coolness and restraint under pressure

---

[31] 4 July 1774, ibid., 228–29.
[32] 20 July 1774, ibid., 233–34.
[33] 24 August 1774, ibid., 241–42.

were for Washington supreme virtues. From him, language like that used to Bryan Fairfax speaks eloquently.

Their conversion to American nationalism came in extraordinary anger, the fury of the jilted lover who is mocked and reviled by the beloved. Lives lived in loyalty to the British Empire, admired by the most Enlightened Europeans for its fusion of power with prosperity and freedom, seemed to crumble in the crisis of 1774, as British behavior finally revealed to the Franklins and the Washingtons how little their loyalty had actually meant. Their reflexive but unnatural solidarity with the Bostonians (about whose motives they still harbored a few doubts), their discovery of all malice and corruption in beloved Britain (not merely Parliament or the King, but Britain) and all virtue in a new American anti-Empire—these were the violent emotional currents behind American revolutionary action, and ultimately behind the attitudes that would make a Federal Constitution possible. If the Republic had finally disintegrated in 1787, their lives would have succumbed to the crisis that had threatened them in 1774.[34]

American nationalism, for them as for thousands of others, was generated by the struggle itself. As in virtually every colonial war for independence in our own time, the war for American independence mobilized support by demanding unity as a necessity for victory, and by justifying unity in terms of the ultimate, ethical goal. In the frenzy of conflict, the American nation became—in the words of a recent student of nationalism—an "imagined community."[35] Almost incidental to the rhetoric of resistance before the outbreak of war in 1775, Americanness became central to any definition of what had been won in 1783, and the loss of American wholeness—whatever might have been preserved of democracy, freedom, or virtue—had come by the 1780s to be equated with Revolutionary failure. As in modern fights for independence, the fight had required the invention of nationalism, and victory had sanctified

---

[34] Of the many accounts of this final crisis of the pre-Revolutionary period, one captures very well a parallel psychological crisis in 1774 among English "radicals," who felt that both the British Empire and the British constitution were collapsing. Colin Bonwick, *English Radicals and the American Revolution* (Chapel Hill, N.C.: University of North Carolina Press, 1977), 67–80. The parallel was pointed out to me by Arlene Phillips Shy.

[35] Benedict Anderson, *Imagined Communities* (London: Verso, 1983). One of the few historians to see and attack the psychological problem posed by rapid conversion to at least a full rejection of Britain, if not fully conscious American nationalism, is Winthrop D. Jordan, "Familial Politics: Thomas Paine and the Killing of the King, 1776," *Journal of American History* 60 (1973), 294–308. Other attempts to get at the psychological basis of the Revolution, emphasizing cultural predisposition and a slower process of alienation, work better for Boston radicals than for the colonies as a whole. Bernard Bailyn, *Ideological Origins of the American Revolution* (New York: Alfred A. Knopf, 1967), and Pauline Maier, *From Resistance to Revolution* (New York: Alfred A. Knopf, 1972).

it, making nationalism a more powerful force—all unintentionally—than the ostensible objects for which independence was originally sought.[36]

* * *

*Robert R. Palmer*. I agree very much with what my friend and one-time colleague Dr. Shy has to say, except I wish we wouldn't use this word "nationalism." It really can mean so many things. I think we're talking about national identity and the gradual process by which it is formed. We had no nation in 1780 but we had *approximately* a process in that direction and the formation of national identity, which we call *national consciousness*. But one thing that I think you might add is that what it consists of is a sense of difference from Europe. I mean, well, not Washington, but Franklin, Jefferson, and Adams had all spent years in Europe. They liked it; they enjoyed it; they admired it. In a way they hated to come home to these simple, primitive conditions. But the more they saw of Europe the more they realized that they were not Europeans and that the Americans were different and that they could never be, as it were, at home permanently in Europe. And the rest of them—Washington—who had never been to Europe were surely a widely read bunch, they read a lot about it and they decided that they would do better—they too were glad they were not Europeans. And I do think this is one of the underlying factors in the formation of a national identity. Otherwise it was a merely pragmatic problem of strengthening the union and how are you going to pay your debts and so forth. I think you wait after Lincoln at the Gettysburg Address. These people in the '80s could not have said, "some such years ago our Fathers brought forth on this continent a new nation." No that was true then. They'd been there since 1640 or so.

*John Shy*. May I simply accept the emendation and addition of not only a friend and former colleague but former teacher—Professor Robert R. Palmer. I agree completely. But let me add something. I think that even Washington, who hadn't been to Europe, had seen a lot of Europeans, between 1775 and 1783 especially, and in varieties of behavior, including the French, who had left him without illusions about what lay on the other side of the Atlantic.

[36] Gerard Chaliand, *Revolution in the Third World* (New York: Viking Press, 1977).

*Speaker Unknown.* Would you expand in a few words on your statement about the Canadian Constitution?

*John Shy.* I had the bad judgment, in the view of some of my colleagues, to start a course in Canadian history at the University of Michigan. It seemed to me that since we were forty miles *north* of Canada at that point that this was an egregious omission. As happens with new courses, whatever the students learn, the teacher learns more. I've been learning things about how the Canadians were putting together their constitution during the 1860s. Actually they were as worried then as they are now about what lies to the south of them, of what this juggernaut, this great North American giant, was likely to do to them, all unintentionally. Clearly they saw the U.S. Constitution as having failed in not effectively subordinating the provinces to the center. That's the most important thing the British North American Act of 1867, once it had put the provincial pieces together (and that was no easy task), was intended to do. Of course the irony, and history is full of ironies, is that today the Canadian federal union seems to be a much weaker, a much less effective federal union than the United States; but that's a subsequent century and more of history that must be examined. But if you look at Canadian intentions in the 1850s and 1860s (and it is the Canadians who put together the British North America Act of 1867, which even today with the Charter of Rights added to it, even in the patriated constitution, is essentially intact)—they intended to avoid the American error of too many compromises—the very thing that had troubled Madison so much when the Virginia plan was rejected. If you look at what Madison said before the convention, and what he did in the convention, there seems to be a change of course during the convention itself. I think he saw the convention, once the Virginia plan had been shot down, as a damage-limiting exercise. That is the view advanced in Harold Schultz's study of Madison, and he persuades me it is correct. The Canadians in the 1860s were trying to keep that from happening.

*Speaker Unknown.* Don't you think the fact that there was a common language had a great deal to do with establishing a national conception?

*John Shy.* It didn't hurt. But not only was there a large part of Pennsylvania that didn't speak English, but another large part of the society had learned English—the Afro-American 20 percent. In the eighteenth century the most massive immigration, except for the Afro-American, was the Scotch-Irish. Even they were looked on as a distinctly different and largely undesirable ethnic group. In legal documents you see references to "thick brogue" and "speaks Irish." I don't want to exaggerate this diversity, but it would be a greater mistake to overemphasize the ethnic homogeneity of American society at that time. As late as 1700 it had still been a fairly homogeneous English society, but great diversification had taken place in just 75 or 80 years.

*Speaker Unknown.* I would like to question whether the most important part of the Constitution to which, I think, no reference has been made in the papers either yesterday or today towards making us a national entity is the commerce clause. I would point out that there is no comparable clause either in the British North America Act of 1867 or in the Australian Constitution Act of 1900, effective in 1901. The commerce clause was the thing that kept us from being Balkanized, and made us a nation.

*John Shy.* Certainly it was very important; it was part of what I referred to as *Realpolitik*—the pragmatic aspect of nationalism. I think the Canadians also tried to do the same thing in the way they specified the division of powers between the provinces and Ottawa. But, alas (and here I think Her Majesty's [later His Majesty's] government have a lot to answer for) they effectively failed; that is, failed in the attempt to give exclusive powers over commerce and interprovincial affairs to the central government. Over time, London gutted these powers of the British North America Act apparently by playing the provinces off against Ottawa, which could be troublesome. Whether London actually intended to do this is not clear. To go back to your original point, I think it has validity.

# "A Vehicle of Life": The Founders' Intentions and American Perceptions of Their Living Constitution

**MICHAEL KAMMEN**

*Newton C. Farr Professor of American History and Culture, Cornell University*

In 1971, when the Judiciary Committee of the United States Senate conducted hearings concerning the nomination of William H. Rehnquist to become an associate justice of the Supreme Court, one senator asked Mr. Rehnquist whether he believed in the concept of a "living Constitution"? The good-natured nominee parried with the quip that a living Constitution was surely more desirable than a dead one. He quickly added, however, that a permanent and stable Constitution seemed preferable to an excessively flexible one that might be rendered less effective by its situational variability.[1]

That seemingly innocent interchange was symptomatic of a significant tension that has been prominent in American constitutionalism for the past sixty years: namely, whether or not ours ought to be, or was meant to be, a "living Constitution." The issue has never been livelier than it is at the present moment. It is important to note, however, that scholars and judges do not agree now any more than they did a generation or two ago, when Professor William W. Crosskey of the University of Chicago Law School, an extremely learned yet peculiarly literal-minded man, fired more than one heavy salvo at the devotees of a "living document."[2]

---

[1]Rehnquist recounted this episode in his essay, "The Notion of a Living Constitution," *Texas Law Review* 54 (May 1976): 693.

[2]See Crosskey, *Politics and the Constitution in the History of the United States* (Chicago: The University of Chicago Press, 1953), 2: 1171–72; Paul Finkelman, "Can We Know the Intentions of the Framers? The Case of the Bank of the United States," *The New Federalist Papers*, 17 April 1986 (no. 114), 3; Herman Belz, "Judicial Power and American Politics: The Original Intention," *The New Federalist Papers*, 9 May 1986 (no. 117), 3.

Even more noteworthy, perhaps, distinguished jurists and the nation's leading law enforcement officials disagree as well. On July 9, 1985, Attorney General Edwin Meese III called for a "jurisprudence of original intention," a position advocated one year earlier from a different perspective by Judge Robert H. Bork of the U.S. Court of Appeals (District of Columbia Circuit).[3] Speeches meant as rebuttals to Meese—and reminiscent in some respects of the didactic role performed by an ancient Greek chorus—by associate justices William J. Brennan and John Paul Stevens have stressed the need for a living Constitution. "The ultimate question must be," Justice Brennan believes, "what do the words of the text mean in our time? "[4]

Although the so-called "Meese–Brennan debate" (a simplistic yet convenient form of shorthand) has received considerable press coverage as well as serious analysis, the attitudes of other justices toward this issue have not been widely noticed. One result is that public perceptions of the polemic tend to assume that two clear-cut positions exist, polar opposites, with no middle ground. Another result is that shades of difference among the more conservative justices—differences that matter—are largely ignored.

We might look, for example, at the views of Justices White and Rehnquist, both of whom in 1973 opposed the majority opinion concerning a woman's right to have an abortion, and both of whom dissented in 1986 when the High Court declared Pennsylvania's Abortion Control Act of 1982 unconstitutional. In his dissent last year, Justice Byron R. White articulated what I would call a carefully modulated, or cautious, affirmation of the living Constitution outlook.

> This Court does not subscribe to the simplistic view that constitutional interpretation can possibly be limited to the "plain meaning" of the Constitution's text or to the subjective intention of the Framers. The Constitution is not a deed setting forth the precise metes and bounds of its subject matter; rather, it is a document announcing fundamental principles in value-laden terms that leave ample scope for the exercise of normative judgment by those charged with interpreting and applying it.[5]

---

[3] Address of Attorney General Meese before the American Bar Association, 9 July 1985, Washington, D.C. (unpublished text courtesy of the Department of Justice), 3, 15; Bork, *Tradition and Morality in Constitutional Law* (Washington, D.C.: American Enterprise Institute, 1984), 11-page address.

[4] Brennan, "The Constitution of the United States: Contemporary Ratification," *The New Federalist Papers*, 29 Nov. 1985 (no. 95), 3–4; Stevens, "The Supreme Court and the Framers," *The New Federalist Papers*, 21 Feb. 1986 (no. 106), 3.

[5] Thornburgh, *Governor of Pennsylvania, et al. v. American College of Obstetricians and Gynecologists, et al.*, 106 S. Ct. 2169 (1986) at 2193–94.

In 1976 Justice Rehnquist published an essay, titled "The Notion of a Living Constitution," which has been cited with some frequency ever since in opinions written by judges at various levels of our legal system. Rehnquist's formulation is more aggressive than White's, and he defends it (with some casuistry, it seems to me) by appealing to democratic theory. Rehnquist basically reifies a straw concept (a caricature of an idea, that is, comparable to a straw man) which he repeatedly refers to as "the brief writer's version of the living Constitution." He argues that, "however socially desirable the goals sought to be advanced by the brief writer's version, advancing them through a freewheeling, non-elected judiciary is quite unacceptable in a democratic society."[6]

Elsewhere in this article, however, Rehnquist pursues a line of argument that lacks intellectual coherence or persuasiveness. Two illustrative sentences may suffice.

- A mere change in public opinion since the adoption of the Constitution, unaccompanied by a constitutional amendment, should not change the meaning of the Constitution.
- The brief writer's version of the living Constitution, in the last analysis, is a formula for an end run around popular government.[7]

I cannot resist the comment that Chief Justice Roger B. Taney's insistence that public opinion as it existed in 1787 must control national jurisprudence in 1857 provided a major prop for Taney's rationale in the disastrous decision concerning *Dred Scott v. Sandford*.[8]

On September 26, 1986, just moments before former Chief Justice Warren E. Burger relinquished his office to Rehnquist, Burger said to four hundred people crammed into the solemn courtroom that justices would always disagree about the meaning of the Constitution; nevertheless, alterations in the Court's composition would not alter its commitment to the U.S. Constitution as "a living document."[9] Using baseball parlance, then, one might say that justices

---

[6] Rehnquist, "Notion of a Living Constitution," 699.

[7] Ibid., 696–97, 706.

[8] See Stanley I. Kutler, ed., *The Supreme Court and the Constitution: Readings in American Constitutional History*, 2d ed. (New York: W. W. Norton & Co., 1977), 152–53.

[9] *New York Times*, 27 Sept. 1986, p. A8. Burger's predecessor, Earl Warren, wrote the following for a lay audience in 1955: "Our judges are not monks or scientists, but participants in the living stream of our national life, steering the law between the dangers of rigidity on the one hand and of formlessness on the other." Warren, "The Law and the Future," *Fortune*, Nov. 1955, 107.

White, Burger, and Rehnquist were playing center, right center, and shallow right field, respectively.

## II

Although the particular phrase "living Constitution" dates largely from the later 1920s and '30s, the general concept first appeared at the turn of the century when a Darwinian notion of our Constitution as a living organism supplanted the popular nineteenth-century metaphor of the Constitution as some sort of mechanism—perhaps even a perpetual-motion machine.[10]

The pivotal figure in proselytizing and popularizing the idea of America's Constitution as a "vehicle of life" was Woodrow Wilson: first as a prolific political scientist, then in lectures and addresses that he gave as the president of Princeton University, and ultimately as governor of New Jersey and as president of the United States. At first he referred to the Constitution's elasticity as its greatest virtue.[11] In 1908, however, when his book *Constitutional Government in the United States* appeared, Wilson worked out a formulation he liked so well that he used it, with only slight variation, three times in the same slim volume. Here is version number three.

> The Constitution cannot be regarded as a mere legal document, to be read as a will or a contract would be. It must, of the necessity of the case, be a vehicle of life. As the life of the nation changes so must the interpretation of the document which contains its change, by a nice adjustment, determined, not by the original intention of those who drew the paper, but by the exigencies and the new aspects of life itself.[12]

After 1920 the revisionist movement known among jurists and scholars as *legal realism* gave great impetus and meaning to the concept of a living Constitution. In an important opinion written for the Court, Justice Oliver Wendell Holmes explained how to handle an issue that is not explicitly dealt with in the Constitution itself.

> The case before us must be considered in the light of our whole experience and not merely in that of what was said a hundred years ago. The treaty

[10] See Michael Kammen, *A Machine That Would Go of Itself: The Constitution in American Culture* (New York: Alfred A. Knopf, 1986), 17–20, 140–41, 177.

[11] Arthur S. Link, ed., *The Papers of Woodrow Wilson* (Princeton, N.J.: . University Press, 1966–), 15: 537; 16: 364; 20: 467.

[12] Wilson, *Constitutional Government in the United States* (New York: Columbia University Press, 1908), 69, 157, 192.

> in question [made in 1916 with Great Britain to protect migratory birds in the United States and Canada] does not contravene any prohibitory words to be found in the Constitution. The only question is whether it is forbidden by some invisible radiation from the general terms of the Tenth Amendment. We must consider what this country has become in deciding what that Amendment has reserved.[13]

Some of the legal realists seemed at least as notable for cynicism as for realism; but following the lead of Benjamin N. Cardozo, venerated as a judge's judge, they gladly rejected the "tyranny of concepts."[14]

The belief that ours is a living Constitution achieved considerable popularity with the lay public during the 1920s and '30s. Newton D. Baker, formerly Woodrow Wilson's Secretary of War, developed the notion in a nationally broadcast speech on Constitution Day in 1932—the very year that H. Arnold Bennett, a prominent authority on constitutional education in the public schools, posed this question: "Are we not a bit too prone to teach the Constitution as a finished document—as the last word in government, as embodying certain principles which under no conditions should be modified?"[15]

Meanwhile, in 1927 Howard Lee McBain, the Ruggles Professor of Constitutional Law at Columbia University, reached out to the mass culture with a compact, easy-to-read book that was part of The World Today Bookshelf, and said on its spine: "Workers Bookshelf." Titled *The Living Constitution: A Consideration of the Realities and Legends of Our Fundamental Law*, it lucidly explained the nature of American government as a whole. What McBain seems to have meant by the phrase "living Constitution" was really a British sort of system, the whole of which completes, alters, and, if necessary, may even override the written document.[16]

During the 1930s, particularly on account of the Great Depression, growing numbers of people came to believe that severe conditions the founders could not have foreseen required a highly adaptable fundamental law. Hence the radical insistence in 1939 by Maury Maverick, a populistic Congressman from San Antonio, Texas, that the Constitution written in 1787 "is not the sole constitution of our American liberties. It is not in itself the Living Constitution, but only a part of it."[17]

---

[13] *State of Missouri v. Holland*, 252 U.S. 416 (1920), at 433–34.

[14] Cardozo, *The Paradoxes of Legal Science* (New York: Columbia University Press, 1928), 60–61.

[15] Kammen, *Machine That Would Go of Itself*, 227, 233.

[16] McBain, *The Living Constitution* (New York: Macmillan, 1927).

[17] See Kammen, *Machine That Would Go of Itself*, 34, 397.

Ever since 1939, however, opinion polls indicate that the general public is far more comfortable contemplating gradual change by fine-tuning rather than any major overhaul in the U.S. Constitution.[18] It is my impression that for more than a generation, now, the idea of a living Constitution has had greater appeal among liberal scholars and social critics than among the public at large.[19]

## III

Given the current absence of consensus, even among constitutional lawyers, judges, and law enforcement officials, it might be meaningful as well as appropriate to ask whether the framers themselves can illuminate the issue? I am not persuaded that a jurisprudence of original intention ought to be the primary criterion in determining whether the concept of a living Constitution deserves an energizing role in American political culture. If the Founders turned out to be categorically opposed to "original intent," however, that would be extremely problematic for proponents of such a position.

The most sensible approach, therefore, is to draw a sampling of their views from a diverse range of ideological and temperamental dispositions. We should start with George Washington, who put his enormous prestige at risk by agreeing to preside over the Philadelphia Convention. Although he felt fully committed to the instrument that resulted, less than two months after the Convention adjourned he wrote the following (in private) to his nephew: "I do not think we are more inspired, have more wisdom—or possess more virtue than those who will come after us."[20] That candid admission surely carried the implication that wise and disinterested citizens might help to execute and even interpret the Constitution in future generations.

Whenever the Convention sat as a committee of the whole, Washington left the chair, joined the Virginia delegation, and the savvy Nathaniel Gorham of Massachusetts presided. Gorham's recognition that any document they fabricated would have to be flexible is clearly reflected in his observation that "the

---

[18] Ibid., 331-32, 383, 388.

[19] See Saul K. Padover, *The Living U.S. Constitution. . . .* (New York: The New American Library, 1953); Arthur Selwyn Miller, *Social Change and Fundamental Law: America's Evolving Constitution* (Westport, Conn.: Greenwood Press, 1979), esp. chap. 1, "The Need for a 'Living' American Constitution," and chap. 10, "Notes on the Concept of the 'Living' Constitution."

[20] Washington to Bushrod Washington, 10 Nov. 1787, in John P. Kaminski and Gaspare J. Saladino, eds., *The Documentary History of the Ratification of the Constitution* (Madison: State Historical Society of Wisconsin, 1976—), 14: 86.

vagueness of the terms constitutes the propriety of them."[21] James Madison, moreover, addressing the Convention, made an unequivocal statement that he and others would subsequently reiterate: "In framing a system which we wish to last for ages, we should not lose sight of the changes that ages will produce."[22]

Alexander Hamilton echoed that sentiment in *Federalist* number 34: "We must bear in mind, that we are not to confine our view to the present period, but to look forward to remote futurity. Constitutions of civil government are not to be framed upon a calculation of existing exigencies; but upon a combination of these, with the probable exigencies of ages, according to the natural and tried course of human affairs."[23] Stephen Cabarrus, a delegate to the ratifying convention in North Carolina, made a similar point more pithily on July 29, 1788: "This is a Constitution for the future government of the United States. It does not look back."[24]

Thomas McKean, who served as Chief Justice of Pennsylvania from 1777 until 1799, worked very actively on behalf of ratification. He reminded members of his state convention that they had under consideration a matter of vast importance, "not only to the present generation, but to posterity."[25] Charles Willson Peale successfully captured that sentiment in his 1787 portrait of McKean and his son, which hangs in the Philadelphia Museum of Art. In addition to the adolescent Thomas, Jr., who obviously represents posterity, the lawyer's table is covered and surrounded by the books and papers of his profession. To complete the symbolism, Peale has placed an allegorical figure of justice, holding her scales and a sword, near the corner of a rooftop that we notice through a window behind the boy's head.

Finally, we should recall the words that Thomas Jefferson wrote to James Madison from Paris in 1789, that "no society can make a perpetual constitution, or even a perpetual law." Jefferson was not present at the Philadelphia Convention, nor can we call his constitutional ideas at all representative. He was a

---

[21] Quoted in Catherine Drinker Bowen, *Miracle at Philadelphia: The Story of the Constitutional Convention, May to September 1787* (Boston: Little, Brown, 1966), 241.

[22] Ibid., 122. For additional evidence of Madison's anticipation of change, future needs, and the wisdom of flexibility, see his remarks on June 22, 1787, in Max Farrand, ed., *The Records of the Federal Convention of 1787*, 2d ed. (New Haven, Conn.: Yale University Press, 1937), 1: 378. A famous passage included by Madison in *Federalist* number 14 certainly suggests that he believed the delegates had been more responsive to present needs than to custom or to the past for its own sake. "Is it not the glory of the people of America," he asked, "that whilst they have paid a decent regard to the opinions of former times and other nations, they have not suffered a blind veneration for antiquity, for custom, or for names, to overrule the suggestions of their own good sense, the knowledge of their own situation, and the lessons of their own experience?" Jacob E. Cooke, ed., *The Federalist* (Middletown, Conn.: Wesleyan University Press, 1961), 88.

[23] Cooke, ed., *The Federalist*, 210.

[24] Jonathan Elliot, comp., *The Debates in the Several State Conventions on the Adoption of the Federal Constitution* . . . 2d ed. (Philadelphia: J. B. Lippincott, 1876), 4: 184. His italics.

[25] Bernard Schwartz, ed., *The Roots of the Bill of Rights* (New York: Chelsea House Publishers, 1971), 3: 640–41.

maverick on these matters, much more radical than his close friend Madison, for example. Nevertheless, Jefferson shared with Chief Justice John Marshall, a political foe whose ideas and tactics he detested, a strong belief in the necessity of a living Constitution—a belief that they both acted upon when they occupied positions of power and responsibility.[26]

Two related points of a more general nature might be mentioned before we move away from the world of the founders. First, as further evidence that they envisioned a living Constitution, consider the momentous matters that they left for the first Congress to resolve. To cite only three of the most weighty: (1) The structure and nature of the entire federal judiciary; (2) What to do about the huge debt that had accumulated under the Confederation government; and (3) Whether to promulgate a Bill of Rights and, if so, what to include?[27] Those were not simply issues appropriate for legislative action. They were constitutional problems; and each one subsequently generated constitutional issues that became highly political as well.

The second point is scarcely new, yet it requires reiteration in this context. Those who signed the Constitution knew that they had been obliged to make a series of compromises, some of which, at the very least, would require major adjustments at some future time. Theodore Roosevelt summarized this imperative extremely well in 1917, and in doing so communicated his own sense of the Constitution as a living entity.

> I am certain that if the people who framed the constitution of the United States, and that was a matter of compromise from first to last, had adjourned midway, and gone back to their respective States to explain the various proposals and why they were for or against this or that proposal, there never would have been a constitution adopted. What they did was to meet, debate, agree, compromise and vote for a constitution. It was a patchwork and it was nothing but compromise. But it has lived, and under it, as interpreted by our Supreme Court, this country has grown to a hundred million, and has fought three small wars, and one of the greatest wars in history, abolished slavery and now, thank God, is taking its part in this war. Even that constitution was reluctantly adopted by the necessary two thirds. But it was put up to them either to take that or anarchy.[28]

---

[26] Jefferson to Madison, 6 Sept. 1789, in Julian P. Boyd, ed., *The Papers of Thomas Jefferson* (Princeton, N.J.: University Press, 1950—), 15: 395–96; Kammen, *A Machine That Would Go of Itself*, 15, 37, 59–60; Francis N. Stites, *John Marshall: Defender of the Constitution* (Boston: Little, Brown, 1981), 98–108, 129-33.

[27] See Charles Warren, "New Light on the History of the Federal Judiciary Act of 1789," *Harvard Law Review* 37 (Nov. 1923): 49–132; Janet A. Riesman, "Money, Credit, and Federalist Political Economy," in Richard Beeman, et al., eds., *Beyond Confederation: Origins of the Constitution and American National Identity* (Chapel Hill: University of North Carolina Press, 1987), 153; Robert Allen Rutland, *The Birth of the Bill of Rights, 1776–1791* (Chapel Hill: University of North Carolina Press, 1955).

[28] Roosevelt to George William Russell, 6 Aug. 1917, in Elting E. Morison, et al., eds., *The Letters of Theodore Roosevelt* (Cambridge, Mass.: Harvard University Press, 1951–54), 8: 1219.

Political anarchy, American style, did occur in 1860–65; and the pertinent point in this context is that extra-constitutional artifices had to be contrived in order to reconcile all the governmental "loose ends" once the fighting stopped. In order to regain admission to the Union, and its seats in Congress, each state that had seceded was required to summon a constitutional convention that would do three things: repeal its act of secession, repudiate the Confederate debt, and abolish slavery in conformity with the Thirteenth Amendment. When the Constitution is silent, creativity becomes inevitable. That is yet another aspect of a living Constitution.

## IV

Although Americans suffered a severe political and constitutional rupture at the time of the Civil War, they subsequently managed to paper it over by means of a judicial fiction, the Supreme Court's decision in the case of *Texas v. White*. As Chief Justice Salmon P. Chase wrote in 1869: "The Constitution, in all its provisions, looks to an indestructible Union, composed of indestructible States."[29] That maxim, and the organicism for which it stands, is yet another aspect of the American commitment to a living Constitution. Combined with the boast that ours is the oldest written national constitution in continuous existence in the world, they have historically sustained more than a modicum of chauvinism along with skepticism concerning the constitutional capabilities of other nations.[30]

Despite admiration for the British constitution expressed by the framers in 1787, it is important to note that having rejected the very concept of an unwritten constitution, Americans deviated a major step further when they affirmed the right to change a written constitution and institutionalized not just one, but several different means of doing so. The method of calling a second constitutional convention has never been tried, even though Jefferson liked the idea as a matter of principle and Abraham Lincoln expressed a preference for it in his First Inaugural Address.[31] James Madison, John Marshall, William Howard Taft, and Warren E. Burger were entirely hostile to

[29] *Texas v. White*, 7 Wallace 700, in Kutler, ed., *The Supreme Court and the Constitution*, 181.

[30] See John Quincy Adams, *An Oration Addressed to the Citizens of the Town of Quincy, on the Fourth of July, 1831. . . .* (Boston: Richardson, Lord and Holbrook, 1831), 32–33.

[31] Willi Paul Adams, *The First American Constitutions: Republican Ideology and the Making of the State Constitutions in the Revolutionary Era* (Chapel Hill: University of North Carolina Press, 1980), 139; Roy P. Basler, ed., *The Collected Works of Abraham Lincoln* (New Brunswick, N.J.: Rutgers University Press, 1953), 4: 270.

the idea; and with every additional year, decade, and century that passes, the likelihood of our ever seeing a second convention recedes.

Although only sixteen amendments have been added since the Bill of Rights was ratified in 1791, the reality remains that our Constitution is a living one—owing above all to the ongoing activity of constitutional interpretation by the U.S. Supreme Court. The number and variety of major theories or concepts that lack intrinsic constitutional validation, yet have acquired it by application and usage, is intriguing. To list only a selection of them may sound like legal mumbo-jumbo to the layman. Nevertheless, it is worth doing in order to drive home the point, in yet another way, that ours has indeed been a living Constitution. The following doctrines have come, and (for the most part) gone. There will be no end of replacements: substantive due process, clear and present danger, preferred freedoms (referring to the First Amendment), ordered liberty, suspect classification, freedom to contract, separate but equal, wall of separation, compelling state interest, the silver platter doctrine, the exclusionary rule, the fair trial doctrine, the special circumstance doctrine, the content neutrality rule, the doctrine of nonsuperfluousness, the fighting words doctrine, and the child-benefit theory.[32]

Should we be dismayed, or even embarrassed, by this plethora of extant and discarded doctrines? Of course not. Such a pattern is the inevitable consequence of our functioning under a fundamental law that is both written and relatively brief. (By comparison, for example, the Constitution of India, prepared in 1949, requires 130 pages [amended through 1963].)[33]

And besides, the necessity for interpretation emerged at the very outset under eminent auspices, to say the least. Late in 1790, Alexander Hamilton, then Secretary of the Treasury, presented Congress with his plan for the establishment of a national bank. President Washington wondered whether such a measure might be illegal, because the Constitution included no provision for Congress to charter a corporation. So he asked Hamilton and Jefferson, the Secretary of State, to prepare opinions in defense of their broad and strict constructionist positions. Hamilton's proved to be the more persuasive, and has been regarded ever since as one of his most brilliant state papers. The core of Hamilton's rationale also contained the seed that would eventually germinate as the concept of a living Constitution.

[32] For explications of quite a few of these doctrines, see Richard C. Cortner, *The Supreme Court and the Second Bill of Rights: The Fourteenth Amendment and the Nationalization of Civil Liberties* (Madison, Wisc.: The University of Wisconsin Press, 1981), 57, 109, 112, 120, 124–25, 133, 177, 186; Judith A. Baer, *Equality Under the Constitution: Reclaiming the Fourteenth Amendment* (Ithaca, NY: Cornell University Press, 1983), 140, 233–34, 276; Carl B. Swisher, *Stephen J. Field: Craftsman of the Law* (Washington, D.C.: The Brookings Institution, 1930), 372–74; Anthony Lewis, *Gideon's Trumpet* (New York: Random House, 1964), 188–89, 191.

[33] See Amos J. Peaselee, ed., *Constitutions of Nations*, 3d ed. (The Hague: Martinus Nijhoff, 1966), 2: 308–438.

> Every power vested in a government is in its nature sovereign, and includes, by force of the term a right to employ all the means requisite and fairly applicable to the attainment of the ends of such power, and which are not precluded by restrictions and exceptions specified in the Constitution, or not immoral, or not contrary to the essential ends of political society. . . . If the end be clearly comprehended within any of the specified powers, and if the measure have an obvious relation to that end, and is not forbidden by any particular provision of the Constitution, it may safely be deemed to come within the compass of the national authority.[34]

A combination of broad construction when appropriate and new amendments when necessary has kept the United States Constitution very much a living charter. Slavery was abolished by amendment. Women were enfranchised by amendment. But racial segregation became unconstitutional by amendment and by judicial interpretation; and by the latter process state legislatures were directed to reapportion their electoral districts so that one person's vote would be worth as much as any other's.

These are all signs of constitutional vitality. It can legitimately be argued that they occurred slowly—much too slowly. For better and for worse, that is the nature of our republican system. Although it may not be swiftly responsive, neither is it precipitous. With a few significant exceptions, such as Prohibition and McCarthyism, the tyranny of public opinion that Tocqueville so feared has not been such a terrible problem, at least not in the realm of constitutionalism. Moreover, public opinion is remarkably resilient. It got us into Prohibition and McCarthyism; but it also got us out.

## V

Having suggested various reasons why the Constitution may properly be considered a living document, and having offered diverse sorts of evidence, I now feel obliged to acknowledge an area of ambiguity. The problem becomes apparent when we compare American attitudes toward the federal Constitution with their state constitutions. We find a curious double standard; for Americans have replaced, revised, and amended their state constitutions much more readily than they have the national charter.

Among the papers of Governor Edmund Randolph of Virginia, there exists the unpublished draft of a national constitution that he prepared in about 1787. The document begins with a general suggestion that we have subsequently been

---

[34] For both positions, see Henry Steele Commager, ed., *Documents of American History*, 7th ed. (New York: Appleton-Century-Crofts, 1963), 156–60, the quotations at 156 and 158. Hamilton's italics.

much more inclined to follow at the federal level. I have in mind Randolph's caution "to insert essential principles only, lest the operations of government should be clogged by rendering those provisions permanent and unalterable which ought to be accommodated to times and events."[35]

A comprehensive history of our state constitutions is neither appropriate nor possible here. Two types of questions, however, are highly germane to the focus of this essay. The first: Have state constitutions been "living constitutions" to the same degree or in the same manner as the federal one? The second: What impact, if any, have our state constitutions, and their interpreters, had upon the "living" attributes of our federal Constitution?

First things first. A tendency developed during the course of the nineteenth century for state constitutions to get longer and longer, like endless freight trains hauling ever larger amounts of ordinary cargo. Ignoring the prescient warning by James Madison that "these political scriptures" should not be too easy to alter or amend,[36] state legislators and voters tended to approve the inclusion of enactments—that is, conventional statutes—that simply did not belong in any text intended to serve as fundamental law. Many of these provisions eventually got to be archaic, with the consequence that too many state constitutions became burdened by the dead hand of the past. Lord Bryce commented upon this phenomenon extensively in his *American Commonwealth*.

> The influences at work, the tendencies which the constitutions of the last forty years reveal, are evidently the same over the whole Union. What are the chief of those tendencies? One is for the constitutions to grow longer. This is an absolutely universal rule. Virginia, for instance, put her first constitution, that of 1776, into four closely printed quarto pages, that is, into about three thousand two hundred words. In 1830, she needed seven pages; in 1850, eighteen pages; in 1870, twenty-one pages, or seventeen thousand words. Texas has doubled the length of her constitution from sixteen quarto pages in 1845 to thirty-four in 1876. Pennsylvania was content in 1776 with a document of eight pages, which for those times was a long one; she now requires twenty-three. The constitution of Illinois filled ten pages in 1818; in 1870 it had swollen to twenty-five. These are fair examples, but the extremes are marked by the constitution of New Hampshire of 1776, which was of about six hundred words (not reckoning the preamble), and the constitution of Missouri of 1875, which has more than twenty-six thousand words. The new constitutions are longer, not only because new topics are taken up and dealt with, but because the old topics are handled in far greater detail. Such matters as education, ordinary private

[35] Moncure D. Conway, *Omitted Chapters of History Disclosed in the Life and Papers of Edmund Randolph* (New York: G. P. Putnam's Sons, 1888), 73–74.

[36] Madison, "Charters, " *National Gazette*, 19 Jan. 1792, in Gaillard Hunt, ed., *The Writings of James Madison* (New York: G. P. Putnam's Sons, 1906), 6: 85.

> law, railroads, State and municipal indebtedness, were either untouched or lightly touched in the earlier instruments. The provisions regarding the judiciary and the legislature, particularly those restricting the power of the latter, have grown far more minute of late years, as abuses of power became more frequent, and the respect for legislative authority less. As the powers of a State legislature are *prima facie* unlimited, these bodies can be restrained only by enumerating the matters withdrawn from their competence, and the list grows always ampler.[37]

In our own time this tendency has become highly problematic. A few state constitutions (such as New Jersey's in 1947 and Virginia's in 1970) have been revised or replaced on a bipartisan basis by very carefully building a consensus and avoiding potentially explosive issues.[38] Other attempts, however, have ended in dismal failure (such as New York's abortive constitution in 1967); and still other attempts are proceeding at this time. According to the chairman of Mississippi's current commission to draft a new state constitution, the state is determined to draw "a new constitutional blueprint that will allow us to face the future instead of hanging on to the past."[39]

The second of my questions—what impact has state constitutionalism had upon federal?—really requires a whole book for an appropriate answer. I shall simply suggest four illustrative themes that might be pursued in order to elucidate the question.

1. There is evidence that passages from the Massachusetts constitution of 1780 anticipated and may have helped to shape the Equal Protection Clause of the Fourteenth Amendment.[40]

2. A reading of the *Federalist* papers suggests that delegates to the Philadelphia Convention in 1787 were aware of certain features in New York's constitution of 1777, and that its successful arrangements provided effective ammunition for advocates of ratification in 1788.[41]

3. So-called "legislative experiments" conducted by the states, particularly during the first third of this century, which were challenged yet

[37] James Bryce, *The American Commonwealth*, 2d ed. (London: Macmillan, 1891), 1: 438–39.

[38] See A. E. Dick Howard, "Constitutional Revision: Virginia and the Nation," *University of Richmond Law Review* 9 (Fall 1974): 1–48.

[39] See Vernon A. O'Rourke and Douglas W. Campbell, *Constitution-Making in a Democracy: Theory and Practice in New York State* (Baltimore: The Johns Hopkins Press, 1943); *New York Times*, 4 April 1964, p. 1; *New York Times*, 8 Nov. 1967, p. 1; *New York Times*, 12 Dec. 1985, p. B25, and 19 Oct. 1986, p. E4.

[40] Ronald M. Peters, Jr., *The Massachusetts Constitution of 1780: A Social Compact* (Amherst: The University of Massachusetts Press, 1978), 196–201; Richard Kluger, *Simple Justice: The History of Brown v. Board of Education and Black America's Struggle for Equality* (New York: Alfred A. Knopf, 1975), 75–76.

[41] See Cooke, ed., *The Federalist*, 167, 328–39, 411, 446, 533, 575.

ultimately received constitutional approval, had a profound effect, in the final analysis, upon both national legislation and constitutional law.[42]

4. In 1977 Justice William J. Brennan asserted that recent adverse decisions by the Supreme Court in the field of civil liberties justified those who are concerned about preserving the achievements of the 1960s in looking more and more to state constitutions for protection. He observed that many state courts already extended to their citizens broader protections than the Supreme Court had held are applicable under the federal Bill of Rights. Brennan lauded the implications of this new state court activism—for a healthy federalism in particular—and others have since noticed the development of a trend, known as "horizontal federalism," in which some of the state supreme courts scrutinize the decisions made by others as carefully as they watch determinations made by the High Court in Washington.[43]

## VI

Some of our most distinguished historians and political scientists have been inclined to minimize the impact of the U.S. Constitution upon American democracy. Frederick Jackson Turner, for instance, once insisted: "Not the Constitution, but free land and an abundance of natural resources open to a fit people, made the democratic type of society in America for three centuries." Robert A. Dahl has provocatively turned the conventional wisdom inside out: "To assume that this country has remained democratic because of its Constitution seems to me an obvious reversal of the relation; it is much more plausible to suppose that the Constitution has remained because our society is essentially democratic."[44]

Once upon a time I found such statements somewhat troublesome—not because they seemed less than reverent, but because the assumptions that

---

[42] For the sheer complexity of this dynamic relationship, see *Bunting v. Oregon*, 243 U.S. 426 (1917); *New State Ice Co. v. Liebmann*, 284 U.S. 262 (1932), covering 262–311 passim; Thomas Reed Powell, "The Supreme Court and State Police Power, 1922–1930," *Virginia Law Review*, vols. 17–19 (1930–33), passim; "Can States Act Without Federal Permission? Dialogue: The Uncertain Status of Federalism," *New York Times*, 16 Nov. 1986, p. E5.

[43] William J. Brennan, "State Constitutions and the Protection of Individual Rights," *Harvard Law Review*, 90 (Jan. 1977): 489–504; "The Emergence of State Constitutional Law," *Texas Law Review* [a symposium issue], 63 (March–April 1985); Robert Pear, "State Courts Move Beyond U.S. Bench in Rights Rulings," *New York Times*, 4 May 1986, p. 1.

[44] Turner, "The West and American Ideals," in Turner, *The Frontier in American History* (New York: Henry Holt, 1920), 293; Dahl, *A Preface to Democratic Theory* (Chicago: University of Chicago Press, 1956), 143.

underpin them have become less valid with the passage of time, thereby leaving their iconoclasm somewhat in limbo—not to mention where it may leave the Constitution. After all, free land and abundant resources have been diminishing, if not vanishing, for a long time now. And various studies have indicated that our society may be less democratic than Dahl would like to believe.

Where, then, does that leave a Constitution that the likes of Turner and Dahl suggest is "merely" an epiphenomenon rather than a prime mover of American democracy? I would answer that question in several ways. First, very few astute observers ever claimed democracy for the Constitution. Perhaps we ought to say that it is neither democratic nor anti-democratic. Rather, both tendencies have in fact flourished under its auspices. Fortunately, because of the value system that we have long subscribed to as a people, the Constitution has been more than compatible with democracy. The two have developed pari passu, with happy consequences for both. Such developments, in my view, would seem to provide important evidence that ours is a living Constitution.

Second, if the Constitution is really based upon popular sovereignty—as the framers claimed in theory, and subsequent implementation over time has augmented in actuality—then it can only be described as a living Constitution. Despite spasmodic resistance, the democratization of American political values has occurred. As presumptions and goals of the populace change, so does the operative nature of the Constitution.

So, perforce, do the views of the ultimate custodians of that Constitution: the U.S. Supreme Court. Justice Harold H. Burton, a moderate Republican politician turned jurist, exemplified that in 1952 when he responded to oral arguments before the Court concerning the issue of racial desegregation. Burton put this question to counsel for the State of Kansas, a man defending the status quo. "Don't you recognize it as possible," Burton asked, "that within seventy-five years the social and economic conditions and the personal relations of the nation may have changed so that what may have been a valid interpretation of them seventy-five years ago would not be a valid interpretation of them constitutionally today?" Subsequently, while interrogating John W. Davis, chief counsel for the "separate-but-equal" defense team, the following interchange occurred.

DAVIS: Changed conditions may affect policy, but changed conditions cannot broaden the terminology of the Constitution. The thought is an administrative or a political one, and not a judicial one.

BURTON: But the Constitution is a living document that must be interpreted in relation to the facts of the time in which it is interpreted.[45]

---

[45] See Kluger, *Simple Justice*, 568, 572–73.

If Burton, who has been described as a fair-minded, middle-of-the-road conservative, could publicly express such a view; and if Justice Lewis F. Powell, a moderate (joined by three others), could conclude an important dissent in 1980 with the reminder to his brethren that "We are construing a living Constitution"; and if the oft-times radical though sometimes unpredictable Hugo Black developed a philosophy of judicial interpretation best defined in terms of the concept of a "living Constitution," then the notion must surely have more substance than shadow, both historically as well as in the present.[46]

And what of the future? As one possible litmus of our living Constitution, I would keep an eye on the notion of "constitutional morality." Although it does not qualify as a familiar household phrase, it recurs with some frequency in the history and language of American constitutionalism. Predictably, perhaps, its meaning has changed over time. When Chancellor Kent of New York used it in 1837, for example, it essentially referred to sanctity of contract—a phase in the intellectual history of property rights and possessive individualism.[47] When Willmoore Kendall used it in 1964, however, he had in mind the assumptions of "Publius" concerning the capacity of the American people for co-operation, self-restraint, and doing what best promotes the true interests of the community.[48]

Although conservative constitutional scholars today tend to reject morality as a proper basis for sound jurisprudence,[49] I wish to close with the prediction that constitutional morality—that is, including social justice and fairness as legitimate criteria—will one day, not far distant, be broadly accepted as an appropriate underpinning for American jurisprudence.[50] Such a prospect would come as no surprise to anyone who has customarily and correctly regarded the U.S. Constitution as a "vehicle of life. "

---

[46] For Burton, see ibid., 610–11; for Powell, see *Rummel v. Estelle, Corrections Director*, 445 U.S. 263 (1980), at 307; and Charles A. Reich, "Mr. Justice Black and the Living Constitution," *Harvard Law Review* 76 (Feb. 1963): 673–754, esp. at 727–50.

[47] See R. Kent Newmyer, *Supreme Court Justice Joseph Story: Statesman of the Old Republic* (Chapel Hill: University of North Carolina Press, 1985), 228, 233.

[48] Kendall, "Constitutional Morality and The Federalist," in Kendall and George W. Carey, *The Basic Symbols of the American Political Tradition* (Baton Rouge: Louisiana State University Press, 1970), 96–118. This posthumously published volume originated as lectures delivered at Vanderbilt University in 1964.

[49] See Henry P. Monaghan, "Our Perfect Constitution," *New York University Law Review* 56 (May 1981): 353–96. But cf. the emphasis upon "general moral purposes" in *The New Right v. the Constitution* (published in 1986 by the CATO Institute), reported in *New York Times*, 7 Aug. 1986, p. A22; and Ronald Dworkin's belief that judicial interpretation is "inevitably a reflection of moral philosophy." Symposium on constitutional interpretation held at Harvard University in September 1986, reported in *Harvard Magazine*, Jan.—Feb. 1987, 52.

[50] See William O. Douglas, *The Right of the People* (Garden City, N.Y.: Doubleday & Co., 1958), 89; "Group Marks 20 Years of Fighting for Rights" [the Center for Constitutional Rights], *New York Times*, 28 Dec. 1986, p. 37.

www.ingramcontent.com/pod-product-compliance
Lightning Source LLC
Chambersburg PA
CBHW061755260326
41914CB00006B/1117
*9781606180747*